FIRST GIRL SCOUT

The Life of

JULIETTE GORDON LOW

by Ginger Wadsworth

Clarion Books

Houghton Mifflin Harcourt

Boston   New York   2012

Clarion Books, 215 Park Avenue South, New York, New York 10003

Copyright © 2012 by Ginger Wadsworth

Clarion Books is an imprint of Houghton Mifflin Harcourt Publishing Company.

www.hmhbooks.com

Text set in Fairfield LH
Book design by Sara Gillingham

Library of Congress Cataloging-in-Publication Data
Wadsworth, Ginger.
First Girl Scout : the life of Juliette Gordon Low / Ginger Wadsworth.
p. cm.
Summary: "Juliette (Daisy) Gordon Low was a remarkable woman with ideas that were ahead of her time. She witnessed important eras in U.S. history, from the Civil War and Reconstruction to westward expansion to post-World War I. And she made history by founding the first national organization to bring girls from all backgrounds into the out-of-doors. Daisy created controversy by encouraging them to prepare not only for traditional homemaking but also for roles as professional women—in the arts, sciences, and business—and for active citizenship outside the home. Her group also welcomed girls with disabilities at a time when they were usually excluded.
Includes author's note, source notes, bibliography, timeline, places to visit, recipes, The Girl Scout Promise and Law, and sheet music for the favorite scout song "Make New Friends.""—Provided by publisher.
ISBN 978-0-547-24394-8 (hardback)
1. Low, Juliette Gordon, 1860-1927—Juvenile literature. 2. Girl Scouts of the United States of America—History—Juvenile literature. 3. Girl Scouts—United States—Biography—Juvenile literature. I. Title.
HS3268.2.L68W33 2012   369.463092—dc22   [B]   2011009642

Images used by permission of the Girl Scouts of the USA are identified at the end of each caption by the following abbreviations:
JGLB—Juliette Gordon Low Birthplace, Savannah, Georgia
NHPC—National Historic Preservation Center, New York City

Manufactured in China
LEO 10 9 8 7 6 5 4 3 2 1
4500311905

For Ann, Gretchen, Bev, Daira, Cheryl,
Barbara, Sandy, Susanna, Heather, Carole, April,
Betty, Sandy, Chrissy, Margo, and the
rest of the gang who belonged to Troop 695.
Friends forever!

CONTENTS

Edward Hughes, a popular London artist, painted this portrait of Juliette Gordon Low. The large oil painting now hangs in the National Portrait Gallery at the Smithsonian Institute in Washington, D.C. *National Portrait Gallery*

ACKNOWLEDGMENTS

AS A WRITER, I rely on e-mail, the Internet, library access, snail mail, and a cell phone, but I can only do so much from my desk in the way of research. I needed to "walk" in Juliette (Daisy) Gordon Low's footsteps as much as possible.

My first trip took me (and my husband, Bill) to Savannah, Georgia, where Daisy was born and raised. The staff at the Juliette Gordon Low Birthplace (JGLB) generously shared Daisy's diary, letters, newspapers, articles, and images with us. The Birthplace is a busy hub! While we worked, the phone rang constantly as people from around the world called to ask questions, arrange visits, and more. Fran Powell Harold, director of the Juliette Gordon Low Birthplace, Katherine K. Keena, program manager, and other staff members graciously helped us despite their hectic schedules.

We toured the Birthplace, both inside and out, and we did additional research at the Georgia Historical Society, also in Savannah. We took a docent-led tour of the Andrew Low House, where Daisy lived as a bride and at the end of her life. The director, Stephen Bohlin, and his assistant, Kate Greene, provided images and relayed answers about the Low House and Daisy's menagerie of pets. Jami Brantley, collections manager/curator at the First Girl Scout Headquarters, answered our many questions when we met her there. Then we went to Laurel Grove Cemetery, where Daisy and her family are buried, and saw Christ Church. Just being in Savannah gave us a rich sense of Daisy's roots.

I went to New York City, where I studied the Juliette Gordon Low archives at the National Historic Preservation Center (NHPC) located within the Girl Scouts of the USA (GSUSA) National Headquarters. Thanks go to Yevgeniya Gribov, archivist, for her enthusiasm and for directing me to relevant materials in their collection.

I traveled to London and saw the spot in Buckingham Palace where Daisy was presented at court, and I walked around Grosvenor Square, where she lived for several years. Exploring London gave me a glimpse into Daisy's world in Great Britain.

In between these trips, I was back in my chair in front of my computer and still relying on many people and sources to help illuminate the countless aspects of Daisy's fascinating life.

Girl Guide experts in Great Britain sent me articles, copies of photographs, and answers to a number of questions. Thank you, Karen Stapley, archivist, and others. From Daniel Scott-Davies, archive and heritage manager of the Scout Association in London, I learned about the formation of the Boy Scouts in Great Britain. Spencer Howard, archivist from the Herbert Hoover Presidential Library in West Branch, Iowa, provided help regarding Lou Henry Hoover. Nora Lewis, director of library and archives at the Georgia Historical Society in Savannah, and other staff members assisted me with image selections and research. Neil Bauman, executive director, and Hugh Hetherington at the Hearing Aid Museum (www.hearingaidmuseum.com) shared helpful information about how Daisy may have coped with her hearing impairment. Carol Johnson loaned me her Girl Scout handbook, and other friends showed me their badges, sashes, and Girl Scout memorabilia and shared remembrances that helped ignite my own fond memories as a Girl Scout and heightened my enthusiasm to "put pen to paper." Staff at the San Diego Girl Scout Council even helped me confirm details of my early days in Girl Scouting.

Lynne Polvino, my editor at Clarion Books, has supported me from day one on this project, and her skillful, insightful editing has richly improved this book. Special thanks go to my husband, Bill Wadsworth. He is not only a great travel partner but a tough and thoughtful editor.

My GSUSA contacts in Savannah and New York continued to answer questions, uncover photos, and provide additional nuggets of information along the way, and I am grateful for their advice and patience. Along with Pamela Cruz, director of the NHPC, Bettye Bradley, vice president of corporate administration, and others, they reviewed the text for accuracy. I did my best to incorporate all their suggestions, and any inaccuracies are mine.

Daisy often traveled back and forth between England and America with her pets, including this beloved parrot, Polly Poons. *Girl Scouts of the USA–JGLB*

INTRODUCTION

AFTER LEAVING GREAT BRITAIN, the ocean liner SS *Arcadian* rocked and rolled in the storm-churned sea. Most of the 320 first-class passengers elected to stay safely in their staterooms . . . except Juliette Gordon Low.

Daisy, as everyone called her, couldn't sit still for long. Instead, she paced the halls of the steamship, trying to sort out her thoughts. A group called the Girl Guides had formed recently in Great Britain, modeled on the worldwide youth movement the Boy Scouts. Daisy had become involved with the young women's organization during her time in Europe, and she liked their emphasis on physical fitness, camping, nature study, first aid, and friendship among girls and women around the world.

During the short year that Daisy had worked with the Girl Guides, she felt that, at long last, she was doing something meaningful. She would be turning fifty-two soon and didn't intend to waste her remaining years. Daisy wanted to bring the Girl Guides to her home country, the United States of America. Long before she sailed for New York, her mind had buzzed with thoughts about how to expand the organization.

Whenever she thought of a new idea, she hurried to her stateroom. Polly Poons, her parrot, squawked in its cage as Daisy picked up her pen and uncapped her bottle of ink. She wrote quickly in her large and loopy penmanship, stringing phrases together like the luminous pearls on her necklace, trying to capture the essence of Girl Guides on paper: *Loving one another . . . lifelong friendship . . .*

helping others . . . spreading goodwill . . . promoting peace. Daisy then added more names to her growing list of friends and influential people to contact once she reached the United States.

She also reread sections of the Girl Guide handbook, *How Girls Can Help to Build Up the Empire,* for inspiration. All across Great Britain, Daisy knew, girls were beginning to meet regularly in their villages or city neighborhoods in small groups called patrols. She had even started three patrols herself. Each patrol, or troop, was named for a flower and had an adult leader. The girls wore uniforms and earned badges with their friends. Daisy loved being part of it all!

With the handbook tucked under her arm, Daisy set off to find General Sir Robert Baden-Powell in the ship's dining room. They had met the year before, in 1911. B-P, as he was called by his close friends and family, was a famous war hero in Great Britain, where Daisy lived most of the time. To Daisy, he was a new friend and a fellow artist who loved children as much as she did.

During his final years as a military man, B-P had founded the Boy Scouts in Great Britain. The organization was so popular that other countries were embracing it too, and B-P was at the start of an international tour to meet new Boy Scouts around the world.

Much to B-P's surprise, thousands of young British girls had written him and asked to join Boy Scouts. B-P felt strongly that there should be two separate groups, one for boys and one for girls. So in 1910 he asked his sister, Agnes Baden-Powell, to head a new organization they called the Girl Guides.

Daisy Gordon Low had offered to help Agnes Baden-Powell. In less than a year's time, Daisy had started Girl Guide troops in Scotland and in London, England, where she maintained homes.

Daisy crossed the Atlantic between England and New York on the SS *Arcadian* several times until the ship was converted to a troop carrier during World War I. In 1917, a German torpedo tore into the ship and sank it. *Ian Boyle/www.simplonpc.co.uk*

She could hardly contain her enthusiasm as her ship docked in New York. While visiting there and in New Jersey, she talked nonstop about the Girl Guides to her friends and relatives. Then Daisy boarded a train for her hometown, Savannah, Georgia.

Daisy was a small woman, but she had the force of a hurricane, and her family and friends knew from experience that she would stir up their daily lives in delightful, unpredictable, and sometimes exasperating ways whenever she returned home. Soon, everyone would learn that Daisy planned to launch the Girl Guides movement in Savannah. But this time, the "hurricane" intended to shake up not just her hometown but the entire country. Daisy had no doubt in her mind that, with her help, the Girl Guides would take root across the United States.

CHAPTER ONE
Love and War Clouds

DAISY'S PARENTS, Eleanor (Nellie) Kinzie and William (Willie) Washington Gordon II, met in the fall of 1853 while Nellie was attending Madame Canda's French School in New York City. One of her friends was Eliza Gordon, a shy girl from Savannah, Georgia. Eliza had two brothers, George and Willie, who were enrolled at nearby Yale University in New Haven, Connecticut. Sometimes, George escorted his sister and her friends to the opera.

Another classmate of Nellie's, Flo Sheffield, lived in New Haven. Flo's parents invited Nellie and Eliza to stay with them over the Christmas holidays in 1853. It would have taken Nellie too long to travel back and forth by train to Chicago, Illinois, her hometown. The three close friends were excited to be together between school terms. They could shop in New York City, go to plays, and enjoy parties under the supervision of Flo's parents. And Eliza's brothers, Willie and George, were staying nearby with cousins, so they would all visit one another.

When Willie came to call on the Sheffields, eighteen-year-old Nellie was not impressed with him. She wrote later that Willie "looked just like a Methodist parson," meaning that he seemed too quiet and reserved. Still, she agreed to let Willie show her around the Yale campus.

At the top of a stairwell in the Yale library, Nellie peered down a shiny, curved wooden banister. She let Willie walk ahead and waited until he reached the bottom of the stairs. Then her tomboy side took over. She slid down the banister, petticoats and skirt aflutter, and landed at Willie's feet. The impetuous act stole the heart of the surprised young Southern gentleman.

Nellie Kinzie was born in Chicago at a time when the young state of Illinois was still part of the "Wild West." Chicago's streets were dirt; the sidewalks were made of wood, and so they were called boardwalks. Only about three thousand people lived there. Out on the prairie nearby, there were wolves, huge herds of buffalo, and other wild animals.

Daisy's mother, Eleanor (Nellie) Lytle Kinzie, was born in 1835. This photograph was taken when she was in her early twenties. *Girl Scouts of the USA-JGLB*

Before coming to Chicago, Nellie's father had been a trapper and an Indian agent at Fort Winnebago, Wisconsin. He was also a silversmith by trade. As an agent, John Kinzie met with many Native American tribes on behalf of the federal government, and he was well respected by the Winnebago, Potawatomi, Chippewa, and Ottawa.

Later, Nellie's father became a bank president, a founder of the Chicago Historical Society, and a toll collector for the Illinois and Michigan Canal. He also helped discover the Ontonagon copper mine in Michigan. Nellie's mother, Juliette Kinzie, published several books about their adventures in the wilderness, which was an unusual accomplishment for a woman at that time.

The Kinzie family lived in a log house near the Chicago River where it emptied into Lake Michigan. They had six sons and one daughter. As a result, Nellie was loved and totally spoiled. She was often allowed to "steal the show" and be the center of attention.

Like the Kinzies, the Gordons were well-established citizens in their community. They lived in a large house that faced a wide boulevard shaded by oaks. Willie's father, William Washington Gordon I, had been the mayor of Savannah and was one of the builders of the Central Railroad and Canal Company. When Willie finished his schooling at Yale, he was expected to return to Savannah.

After their Christmastime meeting, Nellie and Willie began exchanging letters detailing their growing fondness for each other. As Willie Gordon got to know Nellie and learned about her unique upbringing, he fell deeply in love with her. She was different from everyone in his quiet, predictable family. Like her mother, Nellie was a writer. She saved many of the letters she received, kept a diary, and would eventually write a book about her family's history, which she later passed on

Daisy's maternal grandmother, Juliette Kinzie, drew this view of the family's home on the north side of the Chicago River, a short distance from Lake Michigan. It was built in the 1780s by Chicago's first non-native settler. *Author's collection*

to her children. During her courtship with Willie, Nellie wrote to a friend, "I found that I really care more for him [Willie] than for anyone I had ever met."

Years after that first encounter in New Haven, Nellie and Willie became engaged. But before setting a wedding date, they agreed to a compromise on two important issues. Willie was a Presbyterian and Nellie was an Episcopalian, but he agreed to join her church. And Nellie vowed not to criticize slavery, because, after their marriage, she would be living in the South.

After graduating from Yale University, William Gordon joined the cotton brokerage firm of Reed and Tison in Savannah. He served as an officer in the Confederate army during the Civil War. *Girl Scouts of the USA–JGLB*

In the mid-1800s, the economics, ideals and morals, and ways of life differed greatly between the Northern and Southern states. Like most Northerners, Nellie's parents and other relatives favored the growth of cities and depended more on trade than on agriculture. Most Southerners preferred a rural, agricultural life, based on farms and plantations that produced tobacco, cotton, and other field crops. An army of slaves did most of the labor for the larger landholders. After college, Willie became a partner in a Savannah cotton business, and like many Southern businessmen, he owned slaves.

The North opposed slavery; the South supported it. Leaders on both sides worried about how the issue of slavery would be handled in unsettled territories, since pioneers and explorers were pushing westward. Willie and Nellie were well aware of these differences between the regions.

Nonetheless, they were married on December 21, 1857. The newlyweds moved into the Gordon house in Savannah, where they lived with Willie's widowed mother, Sarah.

The Gordons were a serious family, relatives

In 1818, Savannah's mayor, James Moore Wayne, purchased two lots at the corner of Bull and South Broad Streets and built an imposing English Regency–style home on the property. Daisy's grandparents purchased the home in 1831. *Girl Scouts of the USA-JGLB*

recalled, until Willie brought home his lively, quick-tongued Chicago bride. Some even said that things "never were the same in Savannah after Nellie Kinzie Gordon came." This wasn't surprising—in Chicago, Nellie had been the star within her social scene.

Nellie could speak several languages and dazzled everyone with her charm and conversational abilities. Her sharp wit and unexpected remarks added to her appeal. She rode horseback, played the piano, sang, painted pictures, and had boundless energy. Of course, she had been taught all the social skills that daughters from wealthy families were expected to have. But Nellie's behavior wasn't always proper. She cursed from time to time and was described as a "charming mischief-maker."

By the time they had been married three years, Nellie and Willie had two daughters. Eleanor, also called Nell, arrived on September 27, 1858. Juliette Magill Kinzie Gordon was born on Halloween, October 31, 1860, and was named in honor of her Grandmother Kinzie. When she was a baby, an uncle exclaimed, "I bet she's going to be a 'Daisy,'" and the nickname stuck. It soon became clear that Daisy shared many of her mother's personality traits.

The week of Daisy's birth, Abraham Lincoln was elected president of the United States. Lincoln was from Illinois and believed that slavery was morally wrong, and the friction between the North and South had intensified as he campaigned for office. After he was elected, most Southerners did not feel that compromise between the two regions was even possible.

Eleven Southern states, including Georgia, separated from the United States and formed the Confederate States of America. Jefferson Davis, a friend of Willie Gordon's, was elected the first president of the Confederacy. On April 12, 1861, when Daisy was about six months old, shots were fired on Fort Sumter, a Federal (Union) military post, and the war between the North and the South began.

Back in Chicago, Nellie's father and three of her brothers, John Jr., George, and Arthur, heeded President Lincoln's call for soldiers and signed up to support the Union. Meanwhile, Willie Gordon, a proud Southerner, was already enlisted in the Georgia Hussars, a volunteer cavalry militia unit. When it became clear that the war was going to last more than just a few weeks, the Hussars reported for duty in the Confederate army, and Willie was made a second lieutenant. His brother, male cousins, and boyhood friends also joined the Confederate forces. Willie was ordered

Years of strife between the North and the South erupted in civil war when Confederate artillery bombarded Fort Sumter in Charleston Harbor, South Carolina. Union forces occupying the fort surrendered thirty-four hours later, and the Confederate flag was raised. *National Archives*

to Virginia in September 1861 and attached to General J. E. B. Stuart's First Virginia Cavalry regiment of four to five thousand men.

It was a tumultuous and tragic time for the country, as well as for the Kinzie and Gordon families. Nellie Gordon straddled two very different worlds. The Kinzies were Yankees; her new Southern relatives, including her beloved husband, were all Rebels. The Civil War, and its aftermath, would affect every individual in the United States, including little Daisy Gordon.

CHAPTER TWO
The Civil War

NELLIE GORDON stayed with her young daughters in Savannah during the early years of the Civil War. She knew that many residents distrusted her because of her Northern origins and because her father and her brothers were Union soldiers. Some even whispered behind her back that she might be a spy.

Most of the time, Nellie took it in stride. She had other worries, along with everyone else. Because most manufacturing was done in the North, many products, like textiles, were impossible to buy. Confederate paper money became nearly valueless.

Food was scarce too, and as the war progressed, Daisy and her older sister, Nell, grew pale and thin. They only knew about the war in a vague way. It was something really bad, but they were too young to truly understand what was happening in their little world or to the rest of the country.

Nell, who was two years older than Daisy, recalled that Papa and his brother, Uncle George, came home infrequently. Papa would slip into the garden in his tattered gray Confederate uniform and surprise his daughters. He allowed them to help their mother with the dressing of his flesh wounds. Daisy and Nell had no idea at the time that it was not just a game.

Then Mamma's brother, their Uncle John, was killed in battle in 1862. His death devastated the entire Kinzie family, for John was just twenty-three and his wife was expecting their first child. Shortly after John's death, Nellie's two other surviving brothers, George and Arthur, were taken prisoner.

The earliest known photograph of Daisy, taken when she was four or five years old. *Girl Scouts of the USA–JGLB*

While Willie was away with the Confederate troops, Nellie and Grandma Gordon ran the household as best they could, worrying as news of each battle, big or small, reached Savannah. No one was sure exactly where their loved ones might be fighting. Days or weeks could pass before they heard that Willie was still alive, and he was often slightly wounded. Meanwhile, the grim news about other sons and husbands who had been hurt or had died in battle echoed all around them. And of course Nellie also worried about her friends and family who were fighting for the North. She was greatly relieved when she learned that her brothers had been released.

On January 1, 1863, as the country began its third year of civil war, President Abraham Lincoln issued the Emancipation Proclamation, which declared that anyone held as a slave would be free. Although many slaves in the South remained in bondage until the war was over, the proclamation allowed black men to join the Union army or navy. By the end of the war, some 200,000 soldiers and sailors of African descent had fought for the Union. And the Emancipation Proclamation changed the character of the war as federal troops fought even harder to secure a Union victory and freedom for all.

The following month, Willie Gordon was promoted to captain in the Confederate army and was assigned to the staff of General Hugh Mercer, who commanded the District of Georgia.

This map depicts the states circa 1862 during the War of the Rebellion, now commonly called the Civil War. The shaded areas represent the free and border states of the Union. *Library of Congress*

During that summer, the Confederate general Robert E. Lee ordered his Army of Northern Virginia to cross into southern Pennsylvania at Gettysburg, where they faced the Union's Army of the Potomac. Over fifty thousand men died at Gettysburg during the first three days of July, and Lee's soldiers retreated to Virginia. It was the bloodiest battle of the war.

A second military engagement, which had started on May 18, 1863, unfolded at Vicksburg, Mississippi, along the Mississippi River between Memphis and New Orleans. The Union general Ulysses S. Grant's forces bombarded Vicksburg from the south and east. The fighting lasted six weeks before the Confederate troops, under the leadership of General John Pemberton, surrendered to Grant on July 4, the day after the Battle of Gettysburg ended. It was a dark time for the Confederacy. They had lost two major battles, and the Union had gained control of the Mississippi River.

That August, Mamma had a third child, Sarah Alice. Since she shared a first name with her grandmother, Sarah Gordon, her parents called her Alice. Daisy and Nell called her Skinny. They often snuggled in bed with Mamma and their new sister, and for a brief time, they forgot about the Rebels and the scary-sounding Yankees. And they forgot that they were just as skinny as Alice.

In 1864, Yankee troops started to sweep across Georgia. By midsummer, General William Tecumseh Sherman and his men were fighting in the state's capital, Atlanta. Confederate troops were forced to pull back and flee, and the city fell to the Union. As Sherman's men marched on toward the sea and Savannah, they ate all the available food and cut off supplies. Daisy's family, along with the rest of Georgia's residents, was even hungrier than before.

Everyone who worked for the Gordons pitched in to help. They bartered honey for a few precious eggs so that the girls could have enough protein to eat. They buried silver and other family valuables all over the property, knowing that if the Union soldiers came to the Gordon home, they might take anything of value. The grand mahogany furniture was too large to hide, so the family had to hope that the Yankees would not chop it up for firewood. The idea that the approaching army might tramp about the house and garden at any moment must have terrified Daisy and Nell.

The girls may even have heard the sounds of booming guns growing louder as the Northern army pushed closer and closer. Eventually, General Sherman's troops surrounded Savannah. About 250 miles away, Atlanta was still burning. On December 21, 1864, before a single shot was fired inside the city, the mayor of Savannah surrendered. Daisy was four years old.

Long after she grew up, Daisy still vividly remembered the day when General Sherman's army of blue-coated soldiers paraded through the city. The shutters and blinds were closed in the house. Daisy wrote, "I can even now feel the thrill and hear the tramp of the tired troops.

Citizens flee as Sherman's army marches into Savannah. *Georgia Historical Society*

13

My colored nurse waked me from a sound sleep, wrapped me in the blanket of my crib bed, [and] rushed with me to the balcony. . . . I saw for the first time real live Yankees, thousands and thousands of them!" During the procession, a military marching band played a song called "When This Cruel War Is Over."

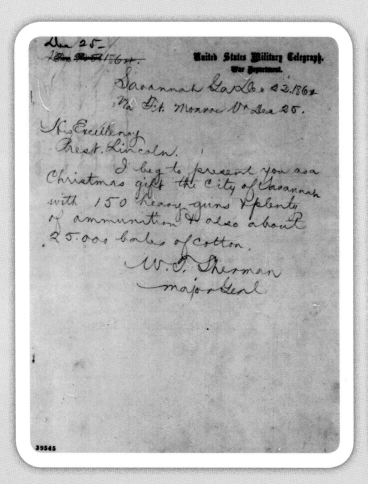

General Sherman's December 1864 telegram to President Lincoln about capturing Savannah, and the first page of Lincoln's response. *Library of Congress*

That week, General Sherman called on Daisy's mother. They had known each other before Nellie Gordon's marriage, and he brought her letters from her family in Chicago and asked if he could help in any way. Sherman was accompanied by a one-armed officer, General Howard, who fascinated Daisy. She wanted to know what had happened. The officer, who missed his own children, set Daisy on his knee and explained that his arm had been shot off by a Rebel's rifle.

"I suppose my father did it," Daisy announced. "He shot lots of Yankees."

Daisy's horrified mother hurried her out of the room.

That night, someone dumped garbage outside the Gordon house to protest that Nellie Gordon had allowed Sherman, the most reviled man in all the South, to step inside her home.

Nonetheless, both generals visited again, bringing candy. Daisy's mother wrote to a friend, "They came to my house frequently and made a great pet of [Daisy], roaring at her comments about Yankees."

Within weeks, General Sherman, following standard wartime procedure, ordered all women who were married to Confederate officers to leave Savannah with their children. He advised Nellie to go to Chicago, and he helped her make arrangements. But Nellie refused to leave without seeing her husband. With Sherman's help, she was able to cross battle lines and meet with Willie one last time in South Carolina. Then, in early 1865, Daisy, Nell, Alice, and their mother took a ship from Hilton Head, South Carolina, to New York City, where they boarded a passenger train for Chicago.

The cars were packed. There wasn't enough room to lie down and sleep, so Daisy and her sisters leaned against their mother for hours. The train was even snowbound

When General Sherman visited the Gordon home, he brought Nell, Daisy, and Alice some rock candy. It was the first sugar the girls had ever eaten. *National Archives*

on the tracks for twenty-four hours between Albany and Buffalo, New York. Union soldiers crowded into each car, singing songs and shouting excitedly to one another. They knew that the war was nearly over and that the North would win.

All the commotion and war talk confused Daisy. She missed home, and especially her father. Yet she wasn't afraid to tell strangers, "I've got a papa down in the Rebel army. I love him *lots!*"

After such a long and uncomfortable journey, the Gordons must have been relieved to finally arrive in Chicago. But almost as soon as she reached her grandparents' home, Daisy fell ill. A doctor was called, and she was diagnosed with what was then called brain fever, which may have been meningitis. Everyone feared that she might die.

CHAPTER THREE
Chicago and Reconstruction

GRADUALLY, DAISY'S FEVER SUBSIDED. The doctors told the family to keep her quiet and calm for the next weeks and months so that the illness would not return. Her worried mother and grandparents, as well as the rest of the family, obeyed the doctor's orders by giving in to her every whim. Slowly, Daisy recovered. A diet of fresh meat and vegetables helped her regain her strength. She ate her first chicken dinner and liked it so much that she repeatedly asked her grandmother to cook "that nice little beefsteak with legs."

Her mother later claimed that during this period her daughter changed from a "sweet and lovely [girl]" into one who was stubborn and refused to listen to reason. Daisy would carry these traits into adulthood and eventually learn to use them to her benefit.

Daisy's grandparents, John and Juliette Kinzie, owned a city block of grass-covered land, which made a perfect play area for her and Nell and Alice. Sometimes,

Native American leaders stopped in Chicago on their way to meet with President Lincoln in Washington, D.C., and they camped on Grandfather's land. Daisy couldn't wait to see her first Indian.

She wasn't disappointed. One day, a party of Winnebago, including a young mother with a papoose on her back, appeared in the garden. Daisy recalled that she and her sister Nell "took up our stand behind a trellis thickly covered with honeysuckle. Here we could see and hear everything. Grandfather sat on a soapbox, the Indians, in a circle, on the ground." Daisy's grandmother served them lemonade and cakes.

"For a long time after they had taken their places, not a word was spoken. . . . At last, the Chief spoke. . . . Then a second Indian spoke . . . and the council continued in just that way until every Indian had spoken and Grandfather had added his opinion at the end."

All that winter and early spring, chatter about the war swirled around the Kinzie household and the neighborhood. It puzzled four-year-old Daisy. Why were people talking about hanging President Jefferson Davis, who was Papa's friend? And why did everyone like Abraham Lincoln? No one liked him in Savannah.

On April 9, 1865, Daisy heard the clanging of cowbells outside. The sounds grew louder and louder. She ran to the front gate to see what was happening. People spilled out of houses into the street, yelling, laughing, and ringing bells. Daisy's grandfather shouted, "The war is over! The war is over!"

Daisy and Nell jumped up and down, crying out, "We've won, we've won!" Grandfather Kinzie kneeled down and explained to his granddaughters in the gentlest way possible that the South had lost. Robert E. Lee, the commanding general of the Confederate army, had surrendered to General Ulysses S. Grant, head of the Union army.

Although he's not in this photo of a Winnebago/Omaha Indian Council meeting, Grandfather Kinzie often met with various tribes to discuss matters such as trade and conflicts with settlers in his role as a United States government Indian agent. He spoke thirteen Native American languages, and some tribes called him Shawniawkie, or "Silver Man," because of the silver ornaments he made and gave to them.
National Anthropological Archives

While sitting on the front gate, Daisy sang "Dixie" as loudly as she could. Passing neighbors laughed and told her that the Confederacy had lost. "Where did it go?" she asked.

Less than a week later, on April 14, 1865, President Abraham Lincoln was shot at Ford's Theater in Washington, D.C., while attending a play. He died the next morning. After the funeral, a train carried Lincoln's body home to Illinois for burial.

All along the 1,600-mile-long train route, hundreds of thousands of mourners—men, women, and children—waited to say goodbye to their president. The Kinzie family must have been in deep mourning too, for they had supported President

Lincoln throughout the Civil War. It was possible that Daisy and her family were among the 125,000 Chicago mourners who paid their respects.

It was also a sad time in the South—they had just lost the war. Daisy's father frequently wrote to his wife from Hillsborough, North Carolina, a town about ten miles from Chapel Hill where he and his company had surrendered. Many of his letters were lost or never arrived, so we don't know if he or Nellie wrote anything to each other about the death of the president. However, Nellie Gordon did receive a letter from Willie dated April 29 saying, "This army has surrendered and the men composing it will be marching to their respective states starting in a few days."

Papa hoped to be allowed to return to Savannah so he could find out whether he could still make a living there. On May 16, he wrote to Nellie, "You'd best stay on in Chicago, till I send for you, for I don't know where to get bread for my mouth and for the present am helpless to fill four or even one more [mouth]. . . . Kiss the chicks [children]."

Before the war, mail delivery had been quick and dependable. Following the war, it was unpredictable. If they arrived at all, letters might reach a large city by train, or a combination of boat and train. In the next weeks and months, there weren't many letters from Papa.

As the country struggled to regroup after the long and divisive war, so did Nellie and Willie. For Willie, it was hard to deal with defeat. He loved the South and the lifestyle he and his parents and grandparents had always enjoyed. It was even harder for him to picture his wife living happily among the conquerors of his army. He longed to hug Nell and Daisy and get to know Alice, who had been born while he was away fighting in the war. It was a dark time in their marriage.

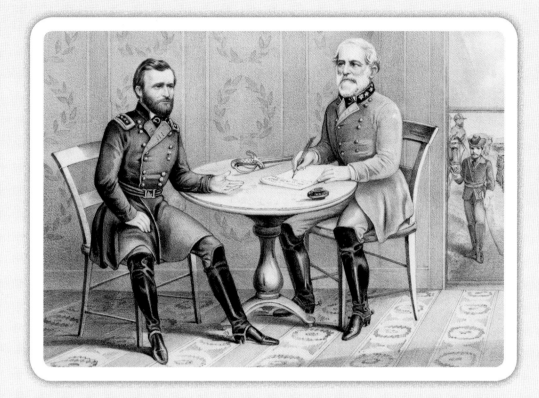

Generals Ulysses S. Grant (left) and Robert E. Lee (right) met at Appomattox Court House, Virginia, to discuss the surrender of the Army of Northern Virginia to end the Civil War. According to the terms, the men of Lee's army could return home in safety if they pledged to end the fighting and deliver their weapons to the Union army. *Library of Congress*

Daisy, her sisters, and their mother stayed in Chicago during the early part of that summer. Throughout those long months, Mamma wrote letter after letter to her husband, with both good and worrisome news, as well as constant assurances that she loved him. But he did not always receive the letters.

If Daisy sensed any tension, she never mentioned it. Instead, she flourished under the loving care of Grandmother Kinzie. "Ganny," as the girls called her, was a spirited yet kind person who was very well educated, especially for a woman of her time. She spoke English, Italian, Spanish, French, and Latin, played the piano, and had finished her schooling at Miss Willard's Troy Female Seminary in New York State.

No doubt, Daisy and Nell begged their grandmother to repeat the stories of her years as a new bride and pioneer, when she married Grandfather Kinzie and traveled west from New York's Hudson Valley to Chicago in a covered wagon, camping in the wilderness and carrying a knife and a tin cup. Their favorite story was about Ganny's mother, Eleanor, who had been kidnapped by a band of Seneca Indians when she was nine. Their great-grandmother lived with the Indians for four years, and because she was a lively girl, the chief called her Little Ship Under Full Sail. Eleanor was eventually returned to her family after the chief saw how much she missed her mother.

Daisy especially loved the "Little Ship" story, and over the years her family called her by that nickname too, because she exuded the same lively energy.

As Daisy, Nell, and Alice recovered from the lean war years and grew strong again, their beloved Grandfather Kinzie was becoming ill and weak, probably with heart-related problems. Willie Gordon had returned to Savannah, and he finally decided that it was time to go north to see his family. To do this, he had to pledge allegiance to the "new" United States.

Daisy's grandmother's book *Wau-Bun* was based on her experiences at Fort Winnebago in what was then the Michigan Territory, and was published in 1856. *Author's collection*

Papa in his Confederate army uniform. *Girl Scouts of the USA-JGLB*

This was not easy for Willie, a former captain in the Confederate army. Still, it gave him the freedom to legally travel beyond Savannah, and he knew his family needed him. He arrived in Chicago shortly after his father-in-law's death in June.

The defeat of the South had left Willie depressed, but being with his wife and three daughters helped lift his spirits. Alice was a busy toddler and no longer thin, although her family would always call her Skinny. Both Nell and Daisy looked tan and healthy. Willie stayed on in Chicago to help settle John Kinzie's business affairs.

Finally, on August 23, 1865, after eight months of being away, the Gordon family returned to Savannah. Mamma rushed inside the house and threw open the shutters. The dusty furniture was still there! Decorative marble mantels stood untouched, and the heavy front doors with their brass fittings were unmarred. Someone had walked through the house, leaving muddy footprints, and most of the kitchenware was gone. But the Gordons were lucky, and they knew it. Throughout the South, many other fine homes and plantations had been damaged or destroyed. Perhaps General Sherman had ordered that their house be protected.

During the war, when most men were off fighting, many women had worked the fields themselves as they struggled to feed and clothe their families. Now the fields surrounding Savannah were thick with weeds. Crops had been eaten by troops, burned, or trampled in battle. The turbulent era of Reconstruction had begun.

Federal troops were present throughout the South to make sure that Southern leaders did not reunite and try to secede again. On December 6, 1865, the necessary number of states ratified the Thirteenth Amendment to the U.S. Constitution, which officially abolished slavery in the United States. Many former slaves moved north to find factory work in the big cities, and some headed west to start over. Others stayed near their homes in the South.

The Civil War left wide swaths of destruction in many areas in the South, as illustrated by this 1865 photograph of Columbia, South Carolina. *National Archives*

Yankees who came to be called carpetbaggers swept into the region, and many literally carried their clothes in inexpensive bags made of carpeting. These outsiders sought political and economic opportunities during this unsettled period and acquired abandoned farms or buildings for just a few dollars in back taxes. Some were honest; most were not.

That first year, the Gordon family focused on restoring their personal property and Papa's business. With lots of scrubbing, followed by new paint on the porch pillars, the house began to look beautiful again. According to one source, Nellie Gordon may have inherited some money from her father's estate or sold some property she owned in Chicago. The money probably helped Willie restart his business, and the family was able to hire some help.

Daisy and Nell were delighted to race around the neighborhood with their cousins, and many of their harsh memories of the war faded. By the following spring, the Gordon girls had a new brother, William Washington, named for their father and grandfather. He had bright red hair and an energetic personality. Everyone loved Willie, or Bill, as he was also called.

And now that she was nearly six years old, Daisy was looking forward to the end of the summer, when she would attend her first real school with Nell.

CHAPTER FOUR

Summers and Schools

AISY'S FIRST SCHOOL was in a house on Hull Street near Chippewa Square. The other students were children from the neighborhood, both boys and girls. Mademoiselle Lucile Blois was their teacher, assisted by her sister, Marguerite. Nell recalled that Mademoiselle Lucile always wore a plum-colored dress, a large gold pin at her throat, and glasses.

Up to this point, Daisy's education had been limited to a short time spent with a governess or whenever an adult could sit down and work with her. The first book she learned to read belonged to her mother and was called *Very Little Tales for Very Little Children.* It was written entirely in single-syllable words.

At the Hull Street school, Daisy and the other new students did lots of repetitive drills, such as copying the same words over and over again from books. She learned quickly in most areas, especially foreign languages. But she was a terrible speller, something even years of schooling and nagging by Mamma would fail to improve. Daisy simply did it her way. She once said, "There's just no use in me having a dictionary. Here I want to know how to spell scent, you know, scent of a flower. And I've looked under *se* and *ce* and it isn't here at all."

Another time, she complained in frustration, "Well, it's not my fault, it's because people drag in such fancy words." Her father was also a poor speller, so perhaps it was an inherited problem. Math challenged Daisy too, and all her life, her family teased her about her difficulties in these two areas.

But during her school years, Daisy discovered something she was really good at: drawing. She was better than anyone else, even the older students. Once, after she received a B in French, Daisy blamed the teacher, who took away points for drawing in class, claiming, "It is hard to pay attention in her stupid old class, but I will try." It wasn't the first time Daisy doodled in school, nor would it be the last.

During those early years following the Civil War, Daisy's family moved back in with her grandmother until they eventually saved enough money to buy a small house down the street. Their cousins, the Andersons, lived next door. The children often gathered under a large pittosporum tree in the garden. With its sturdy, low-hanging branches and dark green leaves, the "spittosporum," as they called it, was a great playground, especially on a hot day.

Sometimes, Daisy and her cousins perched on the branches or pretended that the tree was a house, with imaginary rooms for each child. At Grandmother Gordon's, they raced along the garden paths edged with colorful violets and flowers called snow-drops, hid under tree-shaped camellias, and darted past the carriage house in the back.

The cousins even strung up a sort of communication system between the two houses. Messages swayed back and forth in a basket hung from a sturdy string on a wheel. One read,

This very day at a quarter past three
We all will meet at the Spittosporum tree.

In the late afternoons, Daisy and her siblings and cousins cleaned up and joined Grandmother Gordon for tea. They were expected to be quiet and polite. Despite Mamma's reputation for acting naughty and spoiled when she was young, she demanded proper manners from all her children, as did their grandmother.

Hot, humid summers followed the end of each school year. Before the Civil War, many wealthy families, including the Gordons, would leave the sweltering city of Savannah for an extended vacation. But after the war, Papa, like many of his friends and relatives, was struggling financially and could not afford to take his family out of the city for so long. Planters slowly returned to growing cotton and other crops, and Willie helped them sell their bales of cotton to manufacturers. In time, W. W. Gordon & Co. was again a successful operation.

During the years following the war, though, the family stayed close to home or visited the nearby Isle of Hope, a summer resort, as Willie rebuilt his business. The resort was situated on a tidal river that flowed into the nearby ocean. There were dangerous sharks and rays, so each family used a large bathhouse that jutted out into the salty water, with a partially submerged fence of palmetto boards protecting them. All the children learned to swim at an early age.

Just as businesses and cities were rebuilding during this era of reconstruction, families needed time to mend too. Daisy's parents' relationship had become strained while they were separated, but that time was finally over. Now Mamma and Papa were more in love with each other than ever.

Papa remained loyal to the South and devoted to his family. A calm man, he preferred to sit on the sidelines and enjoy the lively banter between the children and his wife. Mamma adored her husband, and her endless energy and animated personality complemented his steady ways. She kept everyone in the family laughing, whether she was playing the piano, singing, riding horseback, or hosting a dinner party.

Between school terms, the family celebrated the holidays together. On Christmas Eve, everyone squeezed into the library to listen to Papa recite *A Visit from St. Nicholas* by Clement Clarke Moore.

FRANK LESLIE'S ILLUSTRATED NEWSPAPER.

MENDING THE FAMILY KETTLE.

COLUMBIA—"Now, Andy, I wish you and your boys would hurry up that job, because I want to us that kettle right away. You are all talking too much about it."

This 1866 editorial cartoon shows President Andrew Johnson holding a leaking kettle labeled "The Reconstructed South" while a woman with a baby urges him to mend it quickly. The baby represents the newly approved Fourteenth Constitutional Amendment, which provided citizenship to recently freed slaves. The illustration makes a strong political statement while portraying the difficulties families in the South faced during the Reconstruction Era. *Library of Congress*

Then they changed into their nightclothes in front of coal fireplaces in the upstairs bedrooms and tried to drift off to sleep. On Christmas Day, the Gordons opened presents, and the children were allowed to eat dinner with the grownups in the dining room. The day ended with an outing to a Savannah park to enjoy a fireworks display.

The Gordon children grew up loving their parents and loving one another as friends. Daisy was especially close to her father. Besides their problems with spelling, both father and daughter were terrible at keeping track of time and were often late for meals. And they both adored animals.

Mamma didn't share their sentiments, but she tolerated the stray kittens and puppies that Daisy continually brought home. One cold night when she was about eight, Daisy worried about one of the family's cows, so she took some safety pins and a blanket out to the barn and wrapped it up. Another time, she picked up a dog that had been hit by a carriage and that lay on the side of the road. She brought it inside and tried to warm it on a pillow in her mother's bed. Mamma finally convinced Daisy that the dog had been dead for some time. It was no wonder that her brothers and sisters nicknamed her Crazy Daisy!

In 1870 Willie and Nellie finally felt they could afford a family vacation. They traveled north to spend the summer on the south shore of Long Island, New York. The town was called Amagansett, a phonetic interpretation of a native Montaukett Indian word that early colonists took to mean "a place of good water." There were cool breezes and sandy beaches for picnicking and swimming, activities that were popular with many well-to-do families at the time. Mamma believed that breathing the brisk salt air made her children healthier, while swimming made them physically strong. Daisy and her sisters wore swimming outfits that came to their knees and were made of wool or other thick fabric. They were heavy, especially when wet, but a more revealing bathing suit would have been considered immodest. By then, Daisy was already a good swimmer and was used to her attire.

Daisy's Grandmother Kinzie, who still lived in Chicago, joined them on Long Island. Daisy and Nell had remained close to Ganny after their long stay in Chicago at the end of the Civil War. Ganny sent many letters over the years, all addressed to "Miss Juliette Magill Kinzie Gordon." But inside, she always wrote, "My dear little Daisy."

Ganny Kinzie continued to write and publish books. In 1869, J. B. Lippincott Company had published her novel *Walter Ogleby,* which was based on her experiences living in the Hudson Valley in New York State as a young woman. Now, at Amagansett, Ganny was revising a draft of her next book, a novel called *Mark Logan, the Bourgeois.* It was based on the life of the Winnebago chief Red Bird and Ganny's early married life at Fort Winnebago.

Juliette Kinzie was a gentle, devoted grandmother, and she spent plenty of time away from her writing watching Daisy swim and playing with her other grandchildren, Nell, Alice, and Bill. She also fussed over her own daughter, Daisy's mother, who was expecting another baby in October.

A formal portrait of Juliette M. Kinzie, Daisy's maternal grandmother. *Girl Scouts of the USA-JGLB*

Alice, age seven, and Bill, age four, stand on either side of their sister Daisy, who was about ten years old when this photograph was taken. *Girl Scouts of the USA–JGLB*

One September afternoon, Ganny felt she was coming down with a cold. She asked a doctor to send her some cold tablets, which at that time contained quinine. After the unmarked packet of pills arrived, Ganny Kinzie felt hesitant about taking two of them as the doctor had prescribed.

Nellie Gordon encouraged her mother to take them, and she swallowed a pill herself to prove they were safe. Nellie seemed fine, so Ganny took the two pills. Soon, both women felt strange. They grew drowsy and wanted to lie down. Knowing that something was very wrong, Papa sent for a different doctor, who hurried to the house.

The doctor informed them that the pills were not quinine but morphine, a powerful painkiller. Ganny had taken a dangerously high dose, and her body began to shut down. Her breathing slowed, and within four hours, she died.

For the rest of the night, Willie and the doctor walked Daisy's mother up and down the halls of the house. They made her drink strong coffee to keep her awake. Because she had taken a smaller dose of morphine than Ganny, Mamma survived.

No one who was there, including Daisy, would ever forget that long and frightening night. After the tragedy, Willie, always steady and calm, accompanied Ganny Kinzie's body to Chicago so she could be buried beside her husband. The rest of the family returned, grief stricken, to Savannah. On October 28, 1870, Daisy's sister, Mabel McLane Gordon, was born. To everyone's relief, she suffered no problems related to the morphine her mother had taken.

In August 1872, Nellie and Willie had their sixth and last child, George Arthur Gordon, who would go by his middle name, Arthur. The Gordons had strong feelings about the importance of good schooling, and they decided they would pinch pennies and do whatever it took to ensure that all their children continued to be educated after they graduated from the school on Hull Street. They sent their sons, Bill and Arthur, to St. Paul's, a private boarding school in New Hampshire, and then to college at Yale University in Connecticut. Mabel, Alice, Daisy, and Nell went to boarding schools for young women, as was the custom for wealthy nineteenth-century families.

As the oldest, Nell left home for boarding school first. The Virginia Female Institute was in Staunton, Virginia, more than five hundred miles from Savannah. When Daisy was almost thirteen, she claimed she was too big for the little school on Hull Street and insisted on following in her sister's footsteps. Although she was old enough for boarding school, Daisy was physically very small and frail, probably due to the early-childhood illness she suffered in Chicago. Nonetheless, her parents agreed that she could go. Daisy danced about for days, gathering her drawing pads and art supplies and making sure she had packed all her hair ribbons and favorite dresses to take with her on this exciting new experience.

Daisy and her sisters attended several boarding schools, including the Virginia Female Institute, shown here. *Stuart Hall School*

Finally, it was September and time to leave. Daisy kissed Alice, Bill, Mabel, and Arthur goodbye, then hugged her parents and climbed inside the coach with her sister Nell. As the horses trotted down the road to the train station, Daisy decided not to look back for fear that she might cry.

She spent several terms at the Virginia Female Institute (now called Stuart Hall School) and then went on to attend another boarding school, Edgehill, near Charlottesville, Virginia, followed by Miss Emmet's School in Morristown, New Jersey. Like most well-to-do young women of the time, she studied history, English literature, mathematics, natural sciences, Latin, and modern languages. Daisy and her classmates also had moral science classes, where they learned values such as the importance of not lying and how to be respectful toward adults.

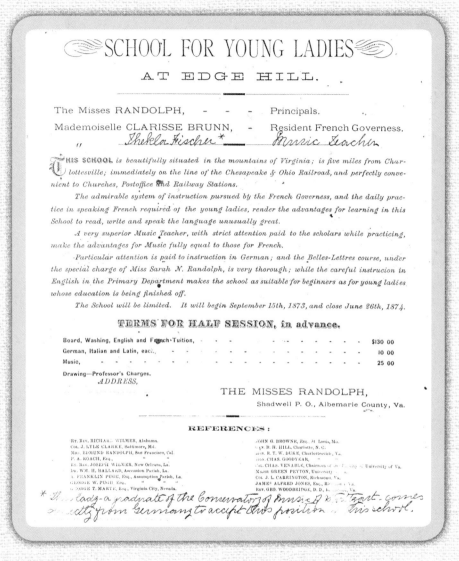

This 1873 advertisement is for one of the boarding schools Daisy attended. It was located in the mountains about five miles from the city of Charlottesville on the Edgehill (sometimes written as Edge Hill) plantation owned by the Randolphs, descendants of Thomas Jefferson. *Virginia Historical Society. Used by permission from the Episcopal Diocese of Virginia.*

Daisy also continued studying art, took horseback riding lessons, and tried ice-skating in the winter. Over the years, she developed an interest in literature and a special fondness for the work of English poets, novelists, and playwrights, including Shakespeare. Her own poetry and prose grew more elegant, though her unpredictable spelling never changed. History, particularly British history, also caught her attention.

While she was away, Daisy received many letters from her parents, especially Mamma, who tried to micromanage her unorganized daughter from Savannah. It seldom worked! Dealing with money was always a challenge for Daisy, and often, the sparks flew between mother and daughter. In one letter to Mamma, she wrote, "Please, don't try to manage *everything* within ten thousand miles of you!" But despite these disagreements, Daisy, like all school boarders, loved getting a box from home filled with candy, cookies, and other treasures.

When Daisy was sixteen, she and Alice spent Christmas in Washington, D.C., with their great-uncle David Hunter and his family. Papa rarely granted his daughters permission to take such trips, so it was a great treat for the sisters. Daisy made all her Christmas presents, including a crayon drawing of a dog, and she stitched a blue fascinator, which was a kind of headpiece with ribbons, bows, and feathers, for a cousin. She wrote home about going to grown-up parties and about meeting cadets from the United States Military Academy at West Point, as well as students from Princeton and Harvard. "I wore my white French muslin overskirt and waist over a black velvit skirt, pink ribbins and my pink roman sash. We had everything good to eat and I ate all day." The friendships Daisy formed with her cousins during the visit would last her entire life.

CHAPTER FIVE

At the Cliffs

T HROUGHOUT DAISY'S CHILDHOOD, the Gordon family would often head "up-the-country," to Etowah Cliffs in the northern part of Georgia, where her Aunt Eliza and Uncle Henry lived. With them went lots and lots of trunks, a governess, and several servants. Eliza and Henry Stiles owned a large house that had been built above the gray cliffs that rose up from the Etowah River. There were long porches called piazzas that faced the water and the sandbars beyond. Behind the house were rose gardens, orchards, and miles and miles of tall pine trees—perfect spots to play and hide. Cartersville, the nearest town, was seven miles away. The surrounding sandy roads were the color of red Georgia soil, and wildflowers bloomed everywhere.

There were several adjoining family properties, so as many as twenty cousins gathered each summer, often with their mothers while some of the fathers stayed behind in hot, muggy Savannah to work.

Daisy loved staying at the Cliffs. There was so much to do!

Daisy cherished her summer stays with her relatives at this big rambling house along the Etowah River in northern Georgia. *Girl Scouts of the USA–JGLB*

The boys had goats that pulled a little cart around the property. Sometimes the girls and boys played together. They might reenact the Civil War, but always with the Confederate army defeating the Yankees. Once, the boys decided Daisy would pretend to be a Yankee spy. They tied her up and stuffed her into a hole in an oak tree. A cousin recalled that Daisy was so small, "only the tip of her sharp little nose could be seen as she tried to peer out from her uncomfortable prison . . . [and] at last her prison-keepers relented and hauled her out."

When the girls tired of playing with the boys, they opened what they called their "circus trunk," which was "filled with a collection of old finery." It was fun to play dress-up, especially on a rainy day.

Their governess taught them in a little schoolhouse under the walnut trees. The children read books with titles like *The History of Sanford and Merton* and *Rollo Learning to Read* that had morals at the end. When she felt rebellious, Daisy would write something silly during their lessons, like this opening stanza from a poem called "The Piggy" that she penned when she was eight or nine years old:

> *I was passing by a pig-sty*
> *When I heard a piggy say,*
> *"I would like to live in rubbish,*
> *Forever and a day."*

As she grew older, though, Daisy seemed to appreciate her summer schooling. When she was thirteen, she wrote in a letter to her mother, who had remained in Savannah,

> *Dear [Mamma],*
> *We have such a nice time up here. . . . We have school till eleven o'clock*
> *in the morning and from half past three till half past four in the evening. I*
> *like the new governess pretty well (but she blew her nose on her dress one*
> *day and so she is not so nice as she was at first, don't tell any body that she*
> *did but she truly did).*

Another favorite pastime at the Cliffs was making taffy from corn syrup, sugar, butter, and molasses. Once the sweet brew had boiled, the cousins let it cool. Then, after coating their hands with butter, they pulled and pulled the taffy into long strands. One time, Daisy let a cousin braid some taffy strands into her hair. The candy hardened and stuck. The only solution was to cut it out!

Daisy liked making paper dolls with her cousin Caroline Stiles. Drawn by Caroline and painted by Daisy, the dolls, which the entire family enjoyed, were copied from a children's magazine. In the years to come, Daisy's and Caroline's little sisters played with them at the Cliffs too.

Left: This page is from the January 1875 issue of *St. Nicholas,* a popular children's magazine. Louisa May Alcott's story *Eight Cousins* was serialized in the magazine and became a constant source of inspiration for the cousins' summertime play. *University of Florida Digital Collection*

Right: On rainy days, Daisy and Caroline made paper dolls, including this one, based on a character in *Eight Cousins. Girl Scouts of the USA-JGLB*

On hot days, the cousins cooled off in the Etowah River. There were sandbars for the smallest children to play on, and farther out, the water was deep enough for swimming. As they waded through the shallows to get there, the older children would often sing loudly.

Each year, Daisy's swimming improved, and over time all the outdoor exercise helped make her less frail. She liked to climb the cliffs beside the river and scale the highest point, Termination Rock, where she could sit and dream up poems or watch birds skim over the water. The children also frequented a site they called the Castle of Redclyffe. Caroline Stiles wrote that the spot "had ledges at various heights for rooms, natural stairways, even a beautiful little tower overlooking the water."

The cousins acted out *The Heir of Redclyffe*, an 1853 novel by Charlotte Yonge, there. Daisy played the main character, Sir Guy Morville, who fell in love with the beautiful Amy but died tragically of a fever at the end of the book. Caroline recalled that everyone "adored acting, with Daisy by far the most gifted among us. She recited well, was a born mimic, and a perfect actress."

The idea to create a literary magazine probably came on a rainy afternoon on one of the big covered porches. Of course, Daisy dove right into this new project. She provided the drawings and even some of her poetry. And with her cousins, she wrote plays, too.

Their drama productions, which were usually held inside Aunt Eliza and Uncle Henry's house, grew more and more elaborate. They put up a sheet to partition off a changing room, where they quickly donned their costumes, all made from items like scarves, veils, and hats found in the big house or taken from the circus trunk.

Daisy's favorite role was Mary, Queen of Scots, which she played in front of a large audience of family members. Using a fake head, the "executioner" beheaded the

reads us out of Willis every sunday and she has read it nearly all through. Antoinne sends her love. I must stop now Good bye your loving little daughter

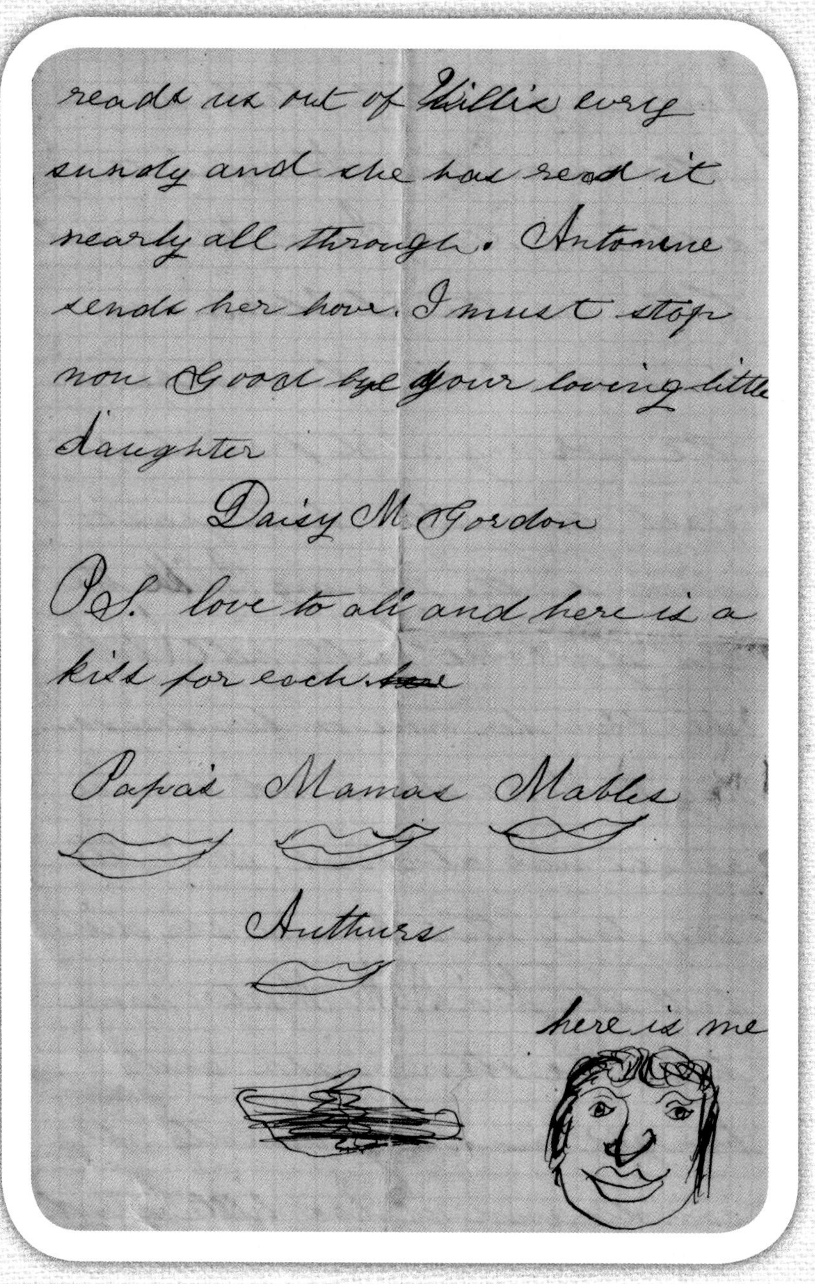

Daisy M Gordon

P.S. love to all and here is a kiss for each.

Papa's   Mama's   Mabels

Authurs

here is me

Daisy ended one letter from the Cliffs with a self-portrait and a hand-drawn kiss for everyone at home: Papa, Mamma, Mabel, and Arthur. *Georgia Historical Society*

Daisy as a young teenager.
Girl Scouts of the USA–JGLB

queen and poured pokeberry juice "blood" all over a white sheet that hid Daisy's real head. It took days to wash the red juice from her hair.

When she was about fourteen, Daisy had her first grown-up visitors at the Cliffs, two West Point cadets. Daisy was in a tree, engrossed in reading *Uncle Silas,* a suspense story by J. Sheridan Le Fanu, when they arrived. She was called back to the house to change into a dress, and her bobbed brown hair was slicked down. As she was ushered into the drawing room, Daisy turned speechless and shy in front of the two young men, and the meeting was disappointing. She later asked her brother Bill if she looked ugly. "Sister, you looked so nice that none of us recognized you," he replied.

One year when she was back home in Savannah, Daisy founded her first club with her cousins and friends. It was called Helpful Hands, and according to Daisy, "its object was to help others." The members decided to sew clothing for needy children, and they picked a local Italian family who ran a fruit stand. They noticed that the children's clothes were nearly threadbare.

Nell later observed that her sister Daisy "did not know how to sew herself!" But that didn't stop her. As Daisy recalled, "Our first job was to make garments. . . . I arranged to give the club instructions in sewing, and collected the members in a circle about me, each one facing me. By mischance I forced them all to thread their needles with their left hands! So we got the name of 'Helpless Hands.'"

The clothes fell apart almost immediately, and the Italian children did not like or wear their new shirts. Still, Daisy recalled how she and the other members "had great fun in [their] club, but it was broken up in the summer of 1876 when the yellow fever epidemic came to Savannah." In fact, later that summer, one member of the Helpful Hands died of the fever; so did one of the Italian children.

Epidemics like yellow fever and malaria often struck Savannah during the hot, oppressive summers. Daisy and her siblings were not allowed to go out in the heat of the day or into the sun without a hat, for fear that they would become ill. Windows stayed closed after dark. Such epidemics were one reason the Gordons and many other well-to-do families fled the city during the summer months. They believed that it wasn't safe to return home until after the first fall frost.

IT IS CONFIDENTLY ASSERTED
THAT
YELLOW FEVER
Can be PREVENTED by the use of
WARNER'S
Safe Kidney & Liver Cure,
in connection with
WARNER'S SAFE PILLS.

All authorities on the subject declare Yellow Fever to be a Blood Poison. The breathing of a malarial infected atmosphere acting directly on the blood.
It is known, admitted, and in writing vouched for, that

Warner's Safe Kidney & Liver Cure

in connection with WARNER'S SAFE PILLS, acting, as it does, directly upon the organs—the Kidneys and Liver—that cleanse and purify the blood, is the best and only effective blood purifier now known.

FOR SALE BY ALL DRUGGISTS.

In the late 1800s, no one knew how yellow fever was transmitted. This advertisement for a preventative pill was published in an 1880 edition of the *National Republican* newspaper. In fact, a vaccine to prevent the disease wasn't developed until 1937, and there is no cure.
Library of Congress

Yellow fever often struck quickly and violently. Patients turned yellowish in color and had a deadly black vomit and a strong odor. No one realized then that yellow fever came from disease-carrying mosquitoes that lived and bred in the surrounding swamps.

In 1876, the disease began to spread throughout Savannah, and Daisy's father decided to stay and help others. He ordered Mamma to take the children to Etowah Cliffs for the summer. And he wrote his will, in case he too caught the yellow fever and died.

The city was divided into districts, and Papa was in charge of one of the largest. After breakfast each morning, he took a quinine pill and a drink of whiskey, a combination that was believed to protect against the illness. Then he set out to help the sick. He called doctors, arranged for food delivery, and visited hospitals. Mamma left her children at the Cliffs under the care of Daisy's Aunt Eliza and nursed friends and families in the nearby Georgia community of Guyton. Mamma had lost a brother, Frank, during Chicago's cholera epidemic of 1850–51 and had firsthand knowledge of how deadly such diseases could be.

It was a long, steamy summer, typical for Savannah and the surrounding areas. Daisy's parents tended to neighbors, servants, friends, and even strangers. Many of them died. By the end of each long day, Willie and Nellie were both exhausted, but luckily, neither one of them came down with the fever.

Meanwhile, Daisy enjoyed another summer at the Cliffs. As an adult, she would return frequently to reminisce about her carefree days spent with her beloved siblings and cousins. Her experiences there—swimming, being outdoors, climbing trees and cliffs, watching birds, gathering wildflowers, writing plays, acting, telling stories, and much more—would strongly influence her life and always stay with her.

Finishing School
CHAPTER SIX

A S EACH SUMMER at the Cliffs drew to an end, Daisy had mixed feelings about returning to Savannah and preparing for the start of school. Trading her relaxed outdoor life for the rigid rules of boarding school was challenging. Being so far away from Mamma and Papa and the rest of the family was also hard. But she liked making new friends, reuniting with old ones, and studying art.

Each fall, Mamma flew into action, ordering the servants to air the trunks and to begin to mend, wash, and press her children's clothes. Before long, Daisy would head down to the train station and return to school.

Instead of going to college, the four Gordon sisters, starting with Nell, would attend a finishing school that was designed to prepare them to be proper young women and wives. Their parents selected Mesdemoiselles Charbonnier's French Protestant Boarding and Day School for Young Ladies in the heart of New York City on East Thirty-sixth Street. All the students studied and spoke in French. Two French

The Gordon children in 1876 (from left to right): Mabel, Nell, Daisy, Arthur, Bill, and Alice. *Girl Scouts of the USA-JGLB*

sisters, Fannie and Mathilde Charbonnier, ran the school, which was nicknamed "the Charbs" by the young women who attended it.

They dressed like French girls, wearing black aprons over their dresses. By the time they graduated, Daisy and her sisters would be fluent in French, literature, grammar, history, and other academic subjects. In addition, they would be well versed in the proper behavior expected of them as they moved into society as single young women.

Daisy and her classmates faced a strict routine. They rose at six in the morning to dress and put their rooms in order. Then they were supposed to study before breakfast, between seven and eight. But Daisy couldn't concentrate; she was always hungry. Admitting that she was also homesick, she wrote, "You don't know how I love you, my dear little Mother! Neither did I until you left me."

Mornings were filled with classes. Daisy couldn't wait for the afternoons, when she could study art. There, she excelled at everything she tried, from drawing with pencil, chalk, or crayon to painting with watercolors. She even painted animals and delicate flowers on dinner plates and teacups.

Dinner was at five thirty. Afterward, the girls studied together in silence in a hall until bedtime. But despite the Charbs' strict schedule, Daisy made many life-long friends. And she managed to enjoy herself. Whenever a package came, the girls sneaked into the school's only bathroom after the Charbonnier sisters were asleep to giggle and share homemade cookies and candy from home.

Daisy's friend Abby Lippitt Hunter later recalled, "There were no games at our school, nor did our teachers think we needed them." Once, she and Daisy and some other girls rushed out into a winter storm to play and throw snowballs at one another. The punishment, staying inside for three entire days, was worth it!

For exercise, their two teachers marched the girls along Madison Avenue in pairs, often en route to Mr. Dodsworth's dancing school at the corner of Twenty-sixth Street and Fifth Avenue. During these walks, they stared at handsome young men and received admiring looks in return. Daisy and her friends also peered into fancy store windows filled with the latest fashions. What she saw inspired her to sketch ideas for hats and gowns during classes and on the edges of letters home.

From an early age, Daisy liked to design her own clothes. She sent sketches to Mamma, with guidelines on how the dress should fit and how many yards of material it would take. *Girl Scouts of the USA–JGLB*

At Mr. Dodsworth's, Daisy learned the minuet, the German, and the court quadrille. But the school provided more than just dance classes. She also learned to enter a ballroom gracefully, to curtsy, and to sit properly—all skills she would use later in life, much to her surprise.

By 1880, Mamma and Papa had moved back into the big house in Savannah and again shared it with Grandmother Gordon. They stayed in touch with their children who were at boarding school by writing frequently, and they expected to hear back on a regular basis. Daisy wrote letters home in French to Arthur and Mabel, who had a French governess. No one was surprised to see that Daisy could not spell any better in French than in English. Yet she somehow managed to win first place for dictation, listening to her teacher speak in French and writing down everything she said, with no spelling errors. Sometimes, Arthur and Mabel's beloved and fun-loving big sister Crazy Daisy baffled them!

When Daisy became one of the older students, she was allowed to leave the Charbs on the weekends to visit cousins or attend the theater or opera, but only with a chaperone. Eventually Daisy earned the daily privilege of leaving school on her own to study oil painting with a famous artist at his studio. Walking back to school one afternoon, she ran into a childhood friend from Savannah, and he walked with her the rest of the way. Daisy said goodbye to him and rushed inside to report herself. Unfortunately, being alone with an unapproved escort, especially a young man, was against the rules. As her friend Abby recalled, "Boys were equally unwelcome either as callers or as escorts."

This photograph of the intersection of Fifth Avenue and Forty-second Street in New York City was taken five years after Daisy left the Charbs, but the scene looks much the same as it did when she and her friends were at school.
Library of Congress

Between terms and in the summers, Daisy returned to Savannah. Rutherford B. Hayes was the president of the United States at the time, and during his presidency the federal troops that had been deployed to the South following the Civil War were removed. Reconstruction was officially over. Now it was up to leaders such as Daisy's father to continue rebuilding the South.

Finished with her education at the Charbs, Daisy's big sister, Nell, was enjoying social life in Savannah. Daisy too would soon complete her formal education and move back to Savannah. Mamma and Papa hoped that their four daughters would marry and start raising families. In Daisy's time, parents expected their daughters to live at home until the right man came along. Moving into an apartment, getting a job, or attending college was practically unheard of. Instead, Mamma and Papa would give them an allowance for clothes, travel, and other expenses. Their sons would go to college and then return to Savannah to work with Papa or to establish their own businesses.

Whenever she was home, Daisy joined Papa for a horseback ride first thing in the morning. Sometimes a dog—often a beagle called Bow-Wow—followed them. Afterward, they turned the horses over to a groomsman at the stable and went inside for breakfast. The cook and her staff prepared the meals in the kitchen, located on the basement level of the house, and sent the food upstairs to the dining room in a dumbwaiter, a small hand-operated elevator. Under Mamma's watchful eye, servants took care of everything in the Gordon household. They also tended the flower-filled gardens and the stable.

When Daisy turned eighteen, she was at the Mesdemoiselles Charbonnier's. She wrote to her father, "Can you realize that just eighteen years ago I was a little red-faced baby?" She reminded Papa that he also said she looked "just precisely like her Ma!"

Daisy's parents agreed that she was finally settling down and growing up. It was time to let her attend parties when she was home. Nell's job was to watch over her sister at these events. The Gordon house was perfect for entertaining. With the furniture pushed to the walls and the mahogany pocket doors between the two adjoining parlors open, the large space made a perfect dance floor. Sometimes Mamma played the piano or hired musicians.

The dancing lessons and manners Daisy learned at the Charbs had often seemed silly, but now she was finally able to put that training to use. Daisy rose gracefully from her chair in the drawing room to meet one dance partner after another and swirl about in an elegant ball gown. It didn't take her long to discover that she would rather dance with a handsome man than with a female classmate.

There had been a time in Daisy's earlier teen years when she had felt rather plain, but now she was a beauty with soft brown curls framing her face. And she was always busy! There was so much to do between school terms. Daisy enjoyed buggy

This lovely portrait of Daisy was taken the year she turned eighteen. *Girl Scouts of the USA–JGLB*

rides, picnics, and boating events with the well-to-do young men and women of Savannah. She was also an excellent horsewoman, and she played tennis. And Daisy loved parties.

Amateur plays, musical presentations, and masquerade balls were popular in the late 1870s. Daisy fit right in. Often cast in the starring roles, she paid close attention to her costumes, just as she did during her childhood days at Etowah Cliffs. Her brother Arthur wryly noted that Daisy "was not only very entertaining and amusing when she desired to be, but she was frequently killingly funny, when she had no intention of being funny at all."

Nell did her best to advise her sister on the rules of etiquette between young single men and women. It didn't always work. When she received her first marriage proposal, Daisy was too naive to know it was even coming. Yet everyone else in her circle of friends seemed to understand that if a single gentleman asked a young woman to walk with him through a cemetery on a Sunday, it meant that he intended to ask her to marry him.

Daisy and her admirer sat on a stone bench in Savannah's Laurel Grove Cemetery. The man told her that he loved her, and he mentioned marriage. Shocked, Daisy jumped to her feet. "How can you so desecrate the dead!" she reportedly said, abruptly ending that relationship.

After a full summer of social events, Daisy returned to the Charbs in 1880 to continue her advanced oil painting lessons. Seventeen-year-old Alice joined her, even though Alice had begged her mother to let her stay at Edgehill in Virginia. It was important to Mamma that all her daughters experience a cosmopolitan city, and become fluent in the French language, as she was.

Alice, seen here, and Daisy shared a room at the Charbs. It was Daisy's responsibility to watch over her homesick little sister. *Girl Scouts of the USA–JGLB*

In early December, Alice came down with a high temperature and a sore throat, followed by a red rash. It was scarlet fever. Daisy didn't believe she'd been exposed to the highly contagious illness. But to be safe, she had to stay away. There were no antibiotics available in 1880 to fight a bacterial infection.

Daisy fretted for days that her sister was sick *and* alone, without any family members to comfort her. Mrs. Gordon came as quickly as possible to Alice's bedside, but the train trip to New York took nearly three days. At first, Alice seemed to improve. The rash went away, but she was still extremely sick. Then on December 30, 1880, Alice died, with Mamma at her side.

Alice was buried in Laurel Grove Cemetery at the edge of Savannah, on a cold, wintry day. Afterward, Daisy stayed home with the family. Mamma blamed herself for forcing Alice to attend school in New York, and she descended into a deep depression. Daisy and Nell mourned too, and they missed the much-needed support of their usually strong and vivacious mother. Like everyone else in the family, they wore black, and as was the custom then, they couldn't attend any social events for a year and a day following Alice's death.

No one—Daisy, her father, or the other children—could break through the thick wall of sadness that surrounded Nellie Gordon. Daisy and Nell spoke in hushed voices around the house for months and months. Sometimes, a single event or memory would stir up emotions, and they cried in one another's arms.

Nine months after Alice's death, Daisy's mother was still inconsolable. Mr. Gordon realized that his daughters were suffering too much. But they did not return to school. Instead, Papa sent them north to New York and New Jersey to stay with aunts, uncles, cousins, and school friends, knowing they would be well chaperoned and taken care of.

It was just what Daisy needed.

CHAPTER SEVEN

Love and Marriage

FROM NEW YORK, Daisy wrote to Grandmother Gordon about the fun of staying up all night, giggling and chatting with her friends and cousins. There were small dinner parties and shopping trips, all appropriately chaperoned by her aunts, uncles, or older cousins. To her grieving mother she wrote, "You probably have not thought my grief profound because I throw it off. . . . It is when I am by myself that I feel it the most. . . . There is more than one kind of sorrow."

Daisy began a pattern of restlessness, of being on the go. In the years ahead, she would frequently travel to New York or New Jersey. There was so much to experience in the New York City area, like the circus, a baseball game, or a clambake at the beach. She even tried and liked canoeing, which was popular with women at that time. Spurred on by Daisy's unique zest for life, her friends and cousins would join her to shop in the city, study the latest fashions, and buy tickets to plays.

Daisy met many unmarried and handsome men in New York as well as in Savannah. Some of her friends, especially those who were Nell's age, were becoming engaged or even getting married.

In 1882, Papa decided that Daisy was ready to tour Europe. Taking an extended trip like this was common for wealthy young women as their formal education came to an end. As she was shopping in New York for the trip and preparing to set sail, Daisy received a telegram from Papa saying that her Grandmother Gordon had died. Daisy was saddened by the loss, but she was even more concerned that her parents, who were still mourning Alice, had to endure yet more grief.

That summer, she went to Europe as planned. She looked forward to exploring historic sites, seeing famous paintings she had studied, and meeting new people along the way.

While in England, Daisy called on her father's colleague Andrew Low, a wealthy cotton merchant who lived in Liverpool and had business interests in Savannah. In fact, Mr. Low had once lived there and still owned a home near the Gordons'. Daisy had a great time exploring the Liverpool area with two of his daughters, Jessie and Mary, and mentioned in a letter home, "I am so glad you and Papa are not like other parents I could mention, 'Andrew' [Low] among them." To Daisy, he seemed old, cranky, and in poor health. Andrew Low's only son, William Mackay Low, was a tall, straight-standing man with thick, curly blond hair and deep blue eyes, handsome enough to be compared to a Greek god by many admiring young women. But Daisy did not mention him in her letters.

However, in the fall, after Daisy had returned from Europe, Willy Low arrived in the United States. He brought her a fox terrier, which was supposedly a gift from Jessie and Mary. Daisy wrote her mother, who was in New York, "He is a dear little dog and I hope you will let me keep him. Willy called the other night and dined here."

Then Daisy joined her mother in Saratoga Springs, a community about two hundred miles north of New York City famous for its many natural mineral springs. Visitors flocked there to soak in the waters, and many believed in their healing powers. It had been nearly two years since Alice's death, and Mrs. Gordon was still devastated. But while in Saratoga Springs, Daisy saw a hint of change in her mother. She wrote her father, telling him, "The waters do her good, she has a splendid appetite.

William Mackay Low was a good-looking man who apparently captured many women's hearts long before he met Daisy. *Girl Scouts of the USA–JGLB*

. . . [But] what pleases me most is that Mam[m]a is so cheery and bright. Don't congratulate her on her improvement, else she will draw into her shell again."

In January 1884, Nell married Wayne Parker, a distant relative, after complaining to Daisy for years that she would surely become an old maid. The ceremony was in Savannah's Christ Church and was followed by a reception at the Gordons' house, which had been spruced up with new carpets and curtains. The wedding celebration seemed to finally lift the family's spirits.

That spring, Daisy decided to return to Europe. She and her father must have talked about Willy Low, because she assured her father that it wasn't likely she would even see him: "[Willy] does not even know that I am coming to Europe, for I have not written to inform him [and] even if I do visit his sisters . . . he is never at home."

Willy Low, as the only male heir to his father's fortune, would someday inherit millions of dollars. To Mr. Gordon, he seemed quite spoiled. Maybe it was because his sisters had raised him after his mother's death when he was a young boy. Papa certainly didn't approve of Willy's flamboyant lifestyle. He was part of the most elite British social circles, followed horseracing, enjoyed hunting, and partied steadily with his friends, such as Albert Edward, the Prince of Wales, who would someday become the king of England. Papa wanted Daisy to marry well, but he strongly believed that all his daughters should seek husbands who supported themselves and their families with hard work. Willy did not work or have any career aspirations.

Daisy had intended to spend time traveling, but instead she stayed with the Lows for much of the summer. "I don't feel in the least afraid of wearing out my welcome because they have made me so much at home that I am like one of themselves," she wrote. Willy Low was definitely around that summer, according to her later correspondence. But Daisy never mentioned him in her letters home at the time.

She did write about visiting many sites, such as Windsor Castle, an enormous medieval structure belonging to the royal family, which she had studied in her English history classes. While exploring Scotland, she reread *The Lady of the Lake*, a book-length narrative poem by Sir Walter Scott set in that country. After the publication of the poem in 1810, Scott's popularity spread beyond Great Britain to the United States, and Daisy had read his poetry in school.

While she was away, Willie Gordon was elected to the Georgia legislature, and she wrote Papa to congratulate him. She also thanked him for the European trip and added, "And now you will probably keep me in this country for the rest of my life and I shall be quite satisfied."

But Daisy was being untruthful. She had fallen in love, yet she knew in her heart that Papa would not approve of William Mackay Low. She did not want to disobey her father. The logical solution, or so it seemed to Daisy, was to never mention Willy in her letters home.

Daisy's diary entries from this time are missing. But her younger sister, Mabel, believed that Daisy and Willy became secretly engaged in 1884, when they were together in England.

It was an awkward period for Daisy's parents as they watched their daughter spurn every other eligible bachelor—and there were many. They worried that Willy Low might break their daughter's heart. There were rumors of other young women he had attracted who had been tossed aside. Yet Willy was the son of a treasured friend and close business associate. They could not turn him away.

In January 1885, Daisy was back in Savannah. Mamma traveled north to Hutton Park, New Jersey, to be with Nell, who was expecting her first baby. When Daisy began to suffer from an earache, she went to a new doctor. As she would later write, "I had [had] a series of ear infections and was losing patience with 'traditional' medicine. I had heard that silver nitrate was the 'newest' treatment." Daisy insisted that the doctor inject her with silver nitrate, which was just beginning to be used as an antiseptic. The doctor refused, but Daisy badgered him until he gave in, injecting it through her nose.

By the time Daisy reached home, the pain was excruciating. Papa reached their regular doctor, who came immediately and administered pain-numbing medication. When Willy Low, who was staying in his father's Savannah home, called on her, Papa would not let him visit her.

Papa wrote Mamma that their daughter's ear was bleeding, possibly from an abscess. He also believed that the silver nitrate, later found to be highly corrosive to cartilage and membranes if given in too high a dosage, was aggravating the situation. Still waiting for Nell's overdue baby to arrive, Mamma wrote back to say that Daisy was pigheaded for seeking such treatment, and then admitted that she was "so nervous to being distracted" because she couldn't help both daughters at the same time.

When Daisy traveled to Europe, she brought several trunks of clothing and was prepared for every occasion.
Girl Scouts of the USA–JGLB

Over the next few days, as the ear discharged more fluid, Daisy's pain subsided considerably. Finally, Papa allowed Willy Low to see her. Nell's baby was born, a twelve-pound girl the proud parents named Alice. And as soon as she could, Mamma hurried home to be with Daisy.

It took months for the pain to go away completely, and Daisy's hearing in that ear was permanently impaired. It was not clear whether it was the original ear infection, the injection, or a combination of both that caused her loss of hearing. But all that time, Willy stayed by Daisy's side, proving to her parents that he loved her.

Willy Low wrote Daisy's father at the end of the year, saying, "My dear Capt. Gordon, . . . Your daughter Daisy and I love one another dearly." Then Willy asked his own father for a bigger yearly allowance, saying he wished to marry her.

By April 1886, Daisy had told her twenty-year-old brother Bill that her future father-in-law had made a generous financial offer to Willy, and he had also promised to fix up the Low home in Savannah for them. Daisy assured Bill, "I am to live in Savannah, so don't fancy we are to be all our lives separated. In summer Willy may want to see his people but our home will be here and even if we go to England it will only be for visits."

In that letter, Daisy mentioned that she and Willy had been in love for years and "as good as engaged" for two years. And now, a radiant Daisy was officially engaged. She picked December 21 for her wedding to Billow, her nickname for her fiancé. She considered the date good luck, since it was also her parents' wedding anniversary.

Although they clearly had some concerns about the upcoming marriage, the Gordons kept their feelings to themselves. Mamma hadn't done much to the house since Alice's death, except to replace old curtains and carpeting and have the interior painted. So she hired a New York architect to create a new look. Starting in early 1886, workers began to construct a third story and a porch on the garden side.

That summer, Billow's father died. Now Billow didn't need to ask for an allowance for himself or his bride-to-be. Unexpectedly inheriting such a fortune may

Beholde ye beauty! — one in three.
Yn Faithe, Yn Hope, Yn Charite

This photo of Mabel, Nell, and Daisy was taken in September 1886. The inscription highlights some of the defining traits of the Gordon family—faith, hope, and charity. *Girl Scouts of the USA-JGLB*

have gone to his head. A few weeks after his father's death, the *New York World* and other newspapers in New York City reported that he had gambled heavily on a polo match. Mr. Gordon could not keep quiet. He wrote Daisy on September 3, 1886, "I am glad Willy was ashamed and indignant at getting in the [news]papers but I think it was his own fault and betting thousands of dollars . . . is neither reputable nor is it calculated to give me confidence to his future."

Nonetheless, the wedding plans moved forward, as did the construction on the Gordon home. In the middle of the project, the contractor in charge died, and the city and surrounding areas experienced a major earthquake, which damaged the house. It took much longer for everything to be completed than anyone had anticipated. But finally, just before the wedding, the work was done and Mamma could instruct the servants to polish every corner of the home from top to bottom.

The morning before the ceremony, Nellie checked every detail one last time. The servants had arranged vases of flowers and lighted fires in the many coal-burning iron fireplaces throughout the house. Then everyone left for the church.

Despite Papa's misgivings about the groom, he escorted his daughter down the aisle and gave her away. At noon on December 21, 1886, Juliette Magill Kinzie Gordon was married to William Mackay Low at Christ Church in Savannah. Ten bridesmaids wearing white silk dresses and plumed bonnets attended the twenty-six-year-old bride.

The event received expansive coverage in the Savannah newspapers, which noted that evergreens and plants decorated the church. Daisy chose a white theme for the wedding, and she carried lilies of the valley, Alice's favorite flower. Since the groom's father had died in July, the white theme was appropriate for mourning.

Wearing a white silk dress with a lace-trimmed train, Daisy added a "sash . . . looped with an elegant crescent of diamonds. Her veil . . . was caught at the side with a diamond star, and she wore a handsome diamond shoulder ornament," a gift from Billow. He picked out the diamonds and designed the silver settings himself.

The newlyweds arrived at the welcoming and warmed house for a midday meal with the immediate family and friends. Afterward, as they hurried out the door to a waiting carriage, Daisy and Billow were showered with rice for good luck. The couple took a boat to St. Catherine's, a barrier island fifty miles south of Savannah off the coast of Georgia, for their honeymoon.

Willy gave each of the bridesmaids a pin in the shape of a daisy, with their wedding year on the stem. The entire pin was encrusted with diamonds.
Girl Scouts of the USA–JGLB

Following their wedding ceremony, Willy and Daisy Low posed with friends and family in the Gordons' garden.
Girl Scouts of the USA—JGLB

Within a day or two, Daisy's good ear began to hurt. Soon, the pain grew un-
bearable, and the couple returned to Savannah to seek medical help. A doctor
removed a grain of rice from Daisy's ear and in the process accidentally punctured
her eardrum and damaged the nerves. From that moment forward, Daisy was totally
deaf in that ear.

CHAPTER EIGHT

Europe

THE NEWLYWEDS SETTLED into the elegant home facing Lafayette Square that Billow had inherited from his father. Under doctor's orders, Daisy lived quietly at first to let her damaged ear heal. She was nearly deaf, but she and Billow were in love, and that was all that mattered.

They filled the house with their wedding gifts, including a floor-to-ceiling gold-framed mirror from the Gordons. With advice and help from her parents, Daisy had the home's interior redecorated. The rooms were freshly painted and wallpapered, and fitted with new rosewood and mahogany furniture that complemented the pieces there that had belonged to Andrew Low. The exterior looked the same then as it does today: stucco over brick, with porches rimmed by fancy iron railings on three sides of the house. A pair of hourglass-shaped flower beds grace the front garden. By the entry stairs, two lion statues stand guard. Daisy liked to pat their heads whenever she went out the front door.

After their wedding, Daisy and Billow lived in this three-story Italianate villa in Savannah. *Library of Congress*

Daisy and Billow began to entertain, and Savannah friends and family looked forward to invitations to the Low house. The centerpiece of their dining room was a Georgian-style mahogany table with a carved base, big enough to seat twenty people. Their Dresden and Spode china and crystal glistened on the white tablecloth. Like her mother, Daisy was a skilled and popular hostess, and she decided not to wallow in self-pity over her hearing loss. Instead, she recognized that "it was simpler to take things into [her] own hands" by being entertaining and witty enough that her guests had to lean in close to hear her every word. She often used an ear trumpet to amplify sounds. Much later, Daisy would look back at this time as one of the happiest years in her life.

But soon Billow grew restless, and Daisy wanted to consult a specialist in England about her hearing condition. The couple prepared to leave Savannah. Servants packed their trunks and Daisy's painting of her mother, and they sailed for England in the spring. Daisy took along her pet mockingbird and the dog Billow's sisters had given her.

At the start of their sea journey, Daisy met an elderly Englishwoman named Lady Bovill, who reminded her of her beloved Grandmother Gordon. Over tea, Daisy admitted that she was nervous about moving so far away from home. The two women chatted comfortably, and Lady Bovill assured Daisy that she would fit easily into English society.

The British Empire was at the peak of its power in 1887, and Daisy and Billow arrived in time to witness a harbor jammed with flag-bedecked military ships and yachts celebrating Queen Victoria's Jubilee, her fiftieth year as the reigning monarch.

Billow's sisters and friends greeted them and made them feel immediately welcome. Within a short time, the newlyweds threw themselves into a fast-paced lifestyle, driven by the personality of Billow's friend Prince Albert Edward of Wales, who enjoyed leisure sports and often invited the Lows to attend events with him. Daisy was not fully prepared to

Knowing that she would live part-time in England in the future, Daisy painted this nearly life-size portrait of her mother to take with her, based on the original by G. P. A. Healy. *Girl Scouts of the USA-JGLB*

step into this society of dukes, duchesses, princesses, and princes who lived in castles and palaces and grand manor houses. While her education was excellent, and her fluent French and knowledge of European history and literature could be put to good use, this was a whole new world. However, after spending time in New York, she felt comfortable in bustling London.

Prince Albert Edward of Wales was Queen Victoria's son and was often called Bertie by his family and close friends. *Author's collection*

The couple slipped easily into an established social scene that revolved around the seasons. They eventually wanted to buy a home, but at first Billow rented a seasonal country property in Warwickshire, outside London. He also took a ten-year lease on a hunting lodge near the Scottish town of Lude in Perthshire, which fed Daisy's lifelong affinity for Scotland. The Lows enjoyed the opera, theater, and city life in London in the summers. During the fall, Billow and Daisy pursued outdoor activities like grouse shooting, deer hunting, and fishing in rural Scotland. Then, after winter arrived, the upper class of England migrated to their country estates. All year long, there were teas and dinner parties, horseraces and fashion shows. Some, like the events at the Ascot Racecourse, were both fashion shows *and* races.

Wherever they lived, there were endless rounds

of themed parties. Some invitations were for fancy costume balls that Daisy adored —she loved to dress up! Many of their friends' large homes and castles had formal ballrooms for dancing. And Daisy was determined not to let her limited hearing be a handicap. She whirled about the dance floors, smiling and laughing with her various partners.

Billow was generous. He gave Daisy more than enough money to buy whatever she wanted, including the latest fashions from Paris. And he enjoyed buying her rubies, diamonds, and sapphires and having them set in designs he personally approved.

In 1889, Daisy and Billow purchased a country estate called Wellesbourne House in the center of Warwickshire, an area known for its excellent fox hunting. Lush lawns surrounded the ivy-covered white stucco home, which became their primary residence.

The property was in a historic part of the English countryside, near Stoneleigh Abbey, a much-larger mansion owned by the author Jane Austen's relatives, the Leighs. At the time, Austen's novels, including *Pride and Prejudice* and *Emma*, were widely read, even though they had been written earlier in the century. Daisy was thrilled to

Daisy always looked elegant. Here, she is dressed in a gown from Paris and wearing diamond swallow-shaped pins that were a gift from Billow. *Girl Scouts of the USA–JGLB*

be close to the Leighs' estate as well as to Stratford-upon-Avon, the birthplace of the playwright William Shakespeare. Castles and large, sprawling homes often were part of the romantic literature Daisy had read as a girl. It was like a dream to be living among them with her handsome husband.

Daisy's pet mockingbird perched on her shoulder while she wrote letters home. "I let him fly about the drawing room and he jumps on my head," she told her mother. "And . . . he scolds and bites my hair, and he snatches the pen from my finger[s] when I try to write." After the mockingbird died, she had her parents send her another one from Georgia.

Although Daisy had promised her brother Bill that she and Billow would live part of the time in Savannah, that was not to be the case. Daisy loved her new life and home. She only managed to return to America in the winter. Her trips there usually consisted of a whirlwind round of visits to her friends and family in the North, time with her parents in Savannah, and, whenever possible, jaunts to Etowah Cliffs, too. Billow joined her on some of these journeys to the United States.

At Wellesbourne House, there were kennels for the hunting dogs. Daisy's growing menagerie of small pet dogs slept on her bed and traveled everywhere with her. They often had funny-sounding names like Blue Blah, a chow, and Chinkapen, a black and white Pekingese. She even laid her pets to rest in a cemetery on the property, where her characteristic misspellings were evident on the tombstones.

Billow stabled fifty horses there, for he liked to go on hunts with hounds and enter steeplechases, horseraces through obstacle courses. Daisy's favorite form of exercise was to ride her horse around Warwickshire. And she and Billow continued to join the Prince of Wales and his friends at racing meets around the country.

Daisy frequently had her picture taken with various pets, including this dog, whose name we don't know. *Girl Scouts of the USA-JGLB*

Eventually, Daisy was invited to appear at court in Buckingham Palace to be presented to Queen Victoria. It was a great honor, and it was important for Daisy, as the wife of an Englishman in high society and an American by birth, that the day go perfectly.

Daisy rushed to Paris and ordered a gown of white satin to be made with a skirt overhung with ostrich feathers and a film of tulle. The dress had three feathers on one shoulder, and its veil with three plumes symbolized the crest of the Prince of Wales. According to court rules, her train had to be over five meters (about sixteen feet) long. It was the most expensive gown Daisy had ever owned! She later wrote, "I wore all my diamonds and carried a white bouquet."

Daisy arrived at the palace at three o'clock in a horse-drawn carriage, accompanied by the Marchioness of Hertford. She waited with hundreds of other invitees and noted, "It took us until six to walk through seven rooms. . . . My train weighed tons and my bouquet pounds! I disposed of the bouquet by perching it on the bustle of the lady in front of me . . . and . . . she carried it the length of all the rooms!" Daisy also mentioned in her letter that she felt a bit like the memorable Becky Sharp in William Thackeray's novel *Vanity Fair* because of the pressing crowd at the palace and that, like Becky, she needed to " 'look out for number one,' " meaning herself.

Queen Victoria spent only an hour receiving guests in the Throne Room, so Daisy did not see her. Instead, she was presented to other members of the royal family and later joked, "I felt exactly as if I were bowing to those wax figures of Royalty at Madame Tussauds and I almost expected to see the ropes of red silk around them and a placard of 'please do not handle the figures.' "

Although Daisy had a happy and busy life, she longed to start a family. And Billow wanted a male heir to carry on his name. But the babies did not come. Daisy quietly consulted doctors to find out why she couldn't get pregnant. According to her sister Mabel, Daisy may have had a miscarriage, but even Mabel didn't know for sure. At that time, no one talked openly about "female issues."

After Daisy seriously injured her back several times while riding her horse, her doctors advised her to give up fox hunting and other strenuous rides that might involve jumping fences or ditches. Even though she could no longer join in, she invited her local fox-hunting friends to her home for lunch or tea after the hunts during the season in Warwickshire.

No one turned down a social event organized by lively Daisy Low. In public, she was always charming and upbeat, despite her personal setbacks, which she tried to keep to herself. Her British friends loved her humorous stories, which were often set in America, and they seldom realized that she had done most of the talking to avoid the strain of trying to hear multiple conversations. At the time, there were several types of ear trumpets, some small enough to fit in a pocket or a purse. No doubt Daisy used one, especially when there might be several people speaking at the same time. Her cook, Mosianna Milledge, who had come from Savannah, often served Southern American food—ham dishes, turtle soup, roasted canvasback ducks, corn, grits, sweet potatoes, and pecan pie—made from produce and meat that Papa sent from home. Daisy kept visitors' books for Wellesbourne House, and they became stuffed with photographs of people and her pet dogs and birds and contained signatures and drawings from family, friends, and dignitaries who visited her from around the world.

Before electrical hearing devices were invented, Daisy used an ear trumpet like these. The stem was inserted into the ear, and the cone was pointed at the source of the sound. The trumpet shape helped amplify the sound and direct it back through the stem and into the ear. Some were made of light metal and others were made of celluloid. *The Hearing Aid Museum/www.hearingaidmuseum.com*

Over the years, Billow continued to join his friends on hunting adventures, and his trips took him farther and farther away, to exotic places like Africa, for big game hunting, and India, where he shot elephants. Meanwhile, Daisy stayed home and kept busy. She carved a mantelpiece to go over the fireplace in Billow's smoking room, where the men gathered after meals to enjoy cigars and play cards. Over the mantel she hung a portrait of Billow painted by James Lynwood Palmer, and she decorated the room with her own oil paintings of some of their best hunting dogs.

This painting by James Lynwood Palmer captured Billow doing one of the things he loved most: riding one of his horses. *Andrew Low House*

Then Daisy took up ironworking, after persuading the village blacksmith to teach her. She had a forge constructed at Wellesbourne, and for an entire summer she hammered away on a pair of iron entrance gates she designed for the house. Her niece, Eleanor, who was twelve at the time and visiting with her mother, Nell, helped "cut from sheets of the copper the flowers and leaves to decorate those gates. The edges were filled; veins were made by hammering them over a grooved instrument; then they were shaped and bent on an anvil." The gates were embellished with daisies. It was hard work, and Daisy commented, "I developed the muscles of my right arm to such an extent that I couldn't get into any of my clothes."

If Daisy was lonely because Billow was away so much, she did not complain until the spring of 1889. Then she wrote Mamma, "One thing I want very much . . . [is] to let Arthur come over and be my guest for the entire summer. I will pay all his expenses. . . . There are many times that I am alone, and if I only had one member of my family with me, I could be so happy."

Mamma agreed to the trip, knowing how much Daisy missed her younger brother. Arthur turned seventeen that August, and the long summer visit would bond brother and sister for the rest of Daisy's life. Nineteen-year-old Mabel also arrived that fall and stayed for a year. She filled her leather-bound diary with snapshots of the house and of friends who visited her sister, and she tucked in newspaper clippings about the times. Mabel had her own bedroom on the second floor, and she visited every summer and for several winters until she married in 1898.

Daisy's parents had visited her in 1887, shortly after her move to England. Three years later, in 1890, she invited them to Wellesbourne House. "I keep thinking all day and dreaming all night of having you and Papa here. Oh! Do try and come. I so long and yearn to see you both." They came the following year, along with Arthur, Mabel, and Bill.

It didn't take Daisy's bubbly, witty Mamma long to become part of Britain's social scene. Friends of Billow and Daisy began to affectionately call them "Puppa" and "Mumma," just as Billow did. Some of them even visited the Gordons in Savannah. Over the years, her parents would return again and again.

Around this time, a new and interesting neighbor moved in nearby. Rudyard Kipling was an author who was just launching his writing career, and he and his American wife, Carrie, visited Wellesbourne often. "Rud" and Daisy shared a fondness for children and animals, and they formed a close friendship.

Although Daisy seemed happy, her relationship with her husband was troubled. Billow had an unpredictable and childish side, and he was often gone for long periods of time. To taunt her, he would speak softly so Daisy couldn't catch every word, and as a result, she was often unsure of his destination or how long he would be away.

After the lease expired on their lodge in Lude, Billow rented a new place, Meallmore Lodge in rugged Invernesshire in the heart of

Daisy's friend Rudyard Kipling was born in Bombay (now Mumbai) and often wrote about India in his short stories and books. His most famous work is *The Jungle Book*, which was published in 1894 and is considered a children's classic today. *Author's collection/Alfred Howes*

the Scottish Highlands, where he hoped he and his friends would have challenging hunting experiences. Seeking adventure had become almost an addiction for him. Daisy had loved going to Lude, and now she looked forward to staying at Meallmore Lodge with her guests.

Billow preferred to hunt in remote countries with just his male friends, so he and Daisy took only one extended international trip together, to Egypt in the late 1880s. In 1895, Daisy took a bold step. This time, it was she who left Billow behind when she departed for Egypt with Mabel. The Gordon sisters were immediately popular with the British officers they met there, after being introduced around by two brothers-in-law of Daisy's longtime friend Abby Lippitt Hunter, whom she knew from the Charbs. They dined with officers every night and toured a remote and dangerous military post at Wadi Halfa in the Nubian Desert. They were the only women there.

They sailed up the Nile, possibly on a dahabeah, a luxurious bargelike vessel with sails that was originally used by Egyptian kings and queens. Mabel and Daisy were also onboard the first boat to ever go over the First Cataract (a series of rapids and small waterfalls at the site of the present-day Aswan Dam), which must have been a thrill. Daisy formed lifelong friendships with several high-ranking British officers during this Egyptian trip, and she was reminded that there were men who lived quite differently from Billow and his social group.

When she returned to England, she found that her relationship with Billow was still strained. Finally, she turned to Mabel and Arthur for advice and support. Daisy wrote Arthur that Billow was "like Scotch weather, when he is bad he is awful, but when really nice, sweeter than summer."

CHAPTER NINE

Wars

DAISY'S PARENTS made plans to come to England in the spring of 1898, but suddenly, war between the United States and Spain loomed. The conflict was mainly over the independence of the small island of Cuba, which Spain had colonized but the United States wanted to liberate. The impending war was based on the Monroe Doctrine, a declaration put forth by President James Monroe in 1823 that the United States would not tolerate a European nation colonizing an independent country in North or South America.

Daisy fretted. What if her father and brothers became involved? She wrote to Arthur, "I think it is all *wrong*. I am miserable about it!"

On February 15, the battleship USS *Maine* exploded and sank in Havana Harbor, Cuba. Two hundred and sixty-six Americans died. President William McKinley demanded that Spain withdraw its forces from the island, but Spain decided to stay and fight. And so the Spanish-American War began in April 1898.

Willie Gordon immediately offered his services to the federal government. The president accepted and made him the brigadier-general representing Georgia. Papa headed to Miami, Florida, to take over his command, the Second Brigade, First Division, Seventh Army Corps. Before long, Bill and Arthur joined him as commissioned officers.

In late January 1898, President McKinley sent the USS *Maine* to patrol the waters near Havana and protect U.S. citizens there. *Library of Congress*

The exact cause of the USS *Maine* explosion was never determined, but the incident inflamed the volatile political situation between Spain and the United States and led to the start of the Spanish-American War. "Remember the *Maine*!" became an American rallying cry. *Library of Congress*

Nellie Gordon followed her husband to Florida too. She visited the troops stationed in the army hospital there and found that thousands of men were ill from drinking polluted water, because at that time Miami was little more than a swamp. The soldiers also didn't have enough food, medicine, blankets, or clean sheets. The conditions were a "positive disgrace," Mamma wrote, and she intended to do something about it.

Daisy loved England, but she considered herself an American first and foremost. As soon as she could, she sailed home to assist her mother, and she arrived in hot and humid Florida that summer.

At first, there wasn't even a kitchen at the hospital, which was made up of a collection of tents. Daisy heated soup on a kerosene stove in the bathroom of her hotel and hauled the hot liquid to the patients. She and her mother made beds, tried to cheer up the sick soldiers, and helped in any way they could.

Many former Confederate soldiers, such as Willie Gordon, volunteered to support their country during the Spanish-American War. Their efforts helped heal some of the remaining rifts between the North and the South. This photograph of Papa was taken while he was training in Savannah before departing for Miami. *Girl Scouts of the USA-JGLB*

The conditions in Miami were quite a contrast for Daisy. Just before sailing for America, she had entertained the Prince of Wales, Lady Randolph Churchill, and other dignitaries at a luncheon at Wellesbourne. Planning the event had been stressful—the menu had to be preapproved by the future king of England, and every aspect of the afternoon needed to be flawlessly executed. One guest arrived early with a roll of red carpet tucked under her arm so the prince could walk on it from his carriage to the house. Daisy was forever grateful to that guest for knowing about this all-important detail of royal etiquette. After everyone had arrived, Daisy relaxed and stepped into one of her favorites roles, enjoying her little party "to her very finger tips." She was especially pleased that Billow was extremely happy that day.

Now Daisy and her mother were busy feeding hard-working soldiers. Finding local eggs, fresh fruit, and vegetables was a constant challenge. One afternoon, after the hospital ran out of milk, Daisy wandered up and down the streets of Miami until she found a cow. Daisy milked the cow, paid for the milk, and carried the brimming bucket back to the hospital tents herself. Mamma wrote proudly, "Daisy is working like a brick."

The Spanish-American War lasted only four months, and no one in the Gordon family actually went into battle. Most of the brief but intense fighting occurred in the Caribbean near Cuba or off the coast of the Philippine Islands, another Spanish colonial possession in the Pacific Ocean. Two major naval battles and several smaller ones destroyed Spain's navy and isolated its troops stationed on the islands. They surrendered to U.S. military forces in August 1898. The war marked a new, dynamic period in the U.S. Navy's history, as well as the rise of the United States as a global military power.

Long before the Treaty of Peace between Spain and the United States was signed in Paris on December 10, 1898, the Gordon family gathered in Savannah for Mabel's wedding to Rowland Leigh, the youngest son of an English nobleman and a relative of Jane Austen's. Rowland's family's ancestral home, Stoneleigh Abbey,

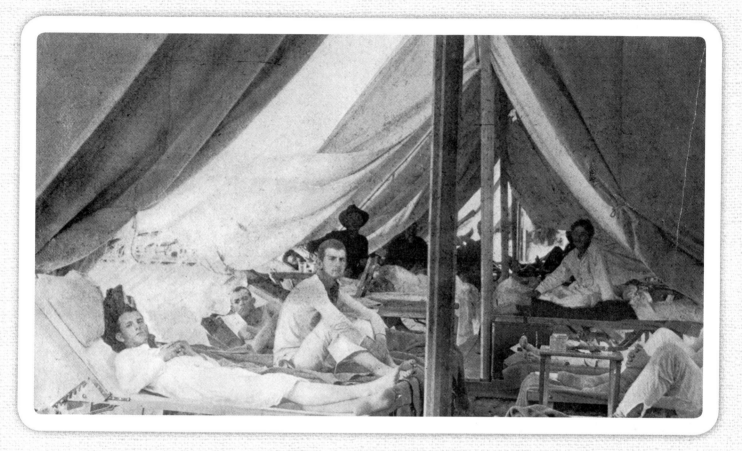

Sick soldiers lay on cots in a temporary hospital at Camp Miami, where Mamma, Daisy, and others helped nurse them. *State Archives of Florida*

was a few miles away from Wellesbourne, on the River Afton, and Mabel had met him while visiting Daisy. The wedding was on October 31, Daisy's thirty-eighth birthday. Rowland had waited nine years for Mabel's father to agree that they could marry. Willie's continuing distrust of Billow made him hesitant to give away another daughter to an Englishman.

After the wedding, Willie and Nellie Gordon, accompanied by the newlyweds, traveled to Washington, D.C. President McKinley greeted them all at the White House and thanked both Gordons for their service to their country.

Daisy returned to England and to her rocky marriage of nearly twelve years. By then, she felt as though she had married a sulking schoolboy who would not grow up. The previous year, Daisy had written to Arthur that when Billow was "annoyed at something, he forgets exactly what it is, but he means to give me a real dressing down."

Daisy had envisioned having the same kind of loving relationship with Billow that her parents enjoyed in their marriage. She wished she could be as strong as her mother, who somehow "managed" Papa without him knowing it. Instead, Billow was in control, and sometimes he taunted Daisy cruelly. Before setting out to meet the Prince of Wales and other friends, he might hint that he would be riding in a dangerous steeplechase horserace. Daisy would not be able to hear most of the details, even with her ear trumpet. Then, while he was away, she would work herself up into a frenzy of worry.

Still, she loved Billow with all her heart, and some friends and family members, Mabel included, felt that he took full advantage of this. He knew that Daisy would always be waiting for him to come home, no matter how long he was away or what he was doing.

Daisy was increasingly lonely. "I see so little of Billow," she wrote Arthur in the summer of 1899, "[that] I feel there is no human affection for me except in the family."

When Nellie and Willie Gordon visited again in 1900, Billow was attentive to them, as always, and Daisy attempted to keep her emotions and problems to herself. But Mamma sensed the rift and began to speak protectively of Daisy as "our Daisy" or "our little Daisy" in letters and in her travel diary.

On January 22, 1901, Queen Victoria died, and Billow's friend Prince Albert Edward became the king of England. Then, Nell's son Wayne fell from a window and died too. Daisy wrote her sister a long letter, saying, "Happiness is not the sum total of life. One's own individual life is such a small part of the working of the big world. . . . [There are] myriad little insects that die to make a coral reef and yet they have their uses and have not lived in vain."

Daisy was alone much of the time that spring. Her marriage all but ended when she learned that Billow had a mistress, a beautiful widow named Anna Bateman. Billow was infatuated with Mrs. Bateman, and by May 1901 they were openly attending parties as a couple and staying in London hotels together. Soon, he moved her into Meallmore Lodge, where he and Daisy lived part of the time, and sent his wife to another wing of their home. Mrs. Bateman even began to order the staff around in Daisy's presence. Instead of behaving like her usual spunky self, Daisy was crushed. She sent for her sister Mabel, who came at once, along with Billow's sister Katy Low.

They left Meallmore for Wellesbourne House so Daisy could pack and return to Savannah. She finally was forced to admit to her parents that her marriage was in shambles. Nellie and Willie Gordon were dismayed for their beloved Daisy but not totally surprised.

By June 1902, Billow had ended the lease on their Scottish lodge and closed Wellesbourne House. Daisy no longer had a home in England or any money.

English friends wrote to tell Daisy that Billow, still living in London, continued to flaunt his relationship with Mrs. Bateman. But Daisy did not want a divorce. She believed that she and Billow had married for life. Plus, she was determined to shield her family from embarrassment. Getting a divorce was scandalous in high society in the early 1900s, and when it did happen, the wife often bore the brunt of the gossip and disgrace.

She told Billow's sisters Katy and Amy that she still loved them, even if they sided with their brother. Katy wrote and said, "How could anyone possibly blame you, dearest Daisy?" His other sisters were equally supportive. Katy Low believed that her brother was drinking himself to death and was not in his right mind.

Daisy decided to return to England to try to deal with the situation. She wasn't sure how she would be received. But to Daisy's surprise, most of their friends supported her, not Billow. Her parents gave her an allowance, but sometimes she ran out of money and was forced to stay with friends.

Finally, Daisy was able to rent a house on Grosvenor Square in London. It was a tumultuous and awkward period in her life. As her brother Arthur noted, his sister was "neither maid, wife, or widow."

Once, Billow stopped by to ask Daisy for a divorce. He was unshaven. His clothes were disheveled and dirty. It was clear that he was terribly ill. A distressed Daisy agreed, but only if Billow would stop drinking and seek medical help. In a letter to Papa, she argued, "Divorce [is] wrong, but it is the lesser of two evils."

The British court system moved slowly forward with the divorce. It was a male-dominated world then, and Daisy relied on her English attorney, Sir George Lewis, and her father to deal with all the legal issues.

Then, in June 1905, Billow Low died. The news saddened Daisy, even though his death was not entirely unexpected. Accompanied by Nell and Mabel, she attended his funeral, which had been arranged by Anna Bateman. She felt she had to go, "for the sake of those years long ago when I loved him."

Daisy had been married nearly nineteen years, and for much of that time, she had lived in Great Britain. Yet when William Low's will was read following the funeral service, it was revealed that he had left almost everything to Mrs. Bateman. Even two of his own sisters, Mary and Jessie, received nothing. Daisy knew this was wrong, and she vowed to have her attorney fight it.

Finally, by November 1906, she was able to write, "All my money bothers are now at an end." Her lawyer had gotten Mary and Jessie a settlement, and Daisy inherited cash, investments, and all of Billow's American possessions, including their home in Savannah. She had cleared the Gordon name. Daisy thanked everyone who had "held out kind hands during the dark years that I now hope are over forever."

She was forty-six years old, and she did not know what she wanted to do with her remaining years. She still traveled regularly and enjoyed parties. Wherever she was—Savannah, New York, London, Scotland, or even in a rented villa—Daisy continually opened her door and her heart to her friends and family.

Peggy Graves, Mabel's daughter, would later reminisce about how her Aunt Daisy would call to say, "Hello Peggy, I have just arrived back—come right over and see me as soon as you can." Daisy's other nieces and nephews also received surprise phone calls and sudden visits from their aunt. They recalled that she smelled of English lavender and French soap and that her trunks were filled with exotic gifts from faraway places. They all expected Aunt Daisy to continue to organize lots of zany and unusual picnics and parties. And she did.

Daisy purchased the house she had been renting at 40 Grosvenor Square in London, as well as the house next door, number 39. Her plan was to live in one house and rent out the other. She loved Savannah, but London offered the theater, opera, and a richer social life. She could shop around the corner on new Bond Street or stroll through Hyde Park. Daisy wanted to put her troubled years behind her, and she seemed to sparkle and laugh more than ever.

Daisy frequented the West End of London, where several theaters were located and the streets bustled with activity. This scene shows Piccadilly Circus and Coventry Street around the time Daisy moved to Grosvenor Square. *Library of Congress*

In central Scotland, she leased a lodge called Lochs in the beautiful valley of Glen Lyon. Daisy especially enjoyed her winter stays there, when snow skimmed the ground. Meggernie Castle, with its towers and window slits in the thick stone walls, loomed nearby. Several ghosts supposedly floated about the halls and rooms at Meggernie, including the spirit of a woman who was murdered—cut in two by her husband. Daisy remained a great storyteller, and she loved to repeat these ghost stories to her visitors at Lochs and to many others who later came into her life.

December 21, 1907, was a bittersweet day. Daisy's parents celebrated their fiftieth wedding anniversary with an elegant party in Savannah. Daisy, Nell, Bill, Mabel, and Arthur wanted it to be a joyous and special event to honor their parents. Daisy dressed in a pale pink gown of old lace covered with coral beads and wore the same diamonds she'd had on when she was presented at the British royal court. Congratulatory gifts and cards flowed in from around the world.

December 21 would have also been Daisy's twenty-first wedding anniversary, as she knew all too well. Late that evening, after the guests left, she grew ill. Despite her frequent travels and busy calendar, unhappiness often swept over her like a fast-moving rain cloud. Being surrounded by her mother, sisters, aunts, female cousins, sisters-in-law, and all their children reminded her even more of her failed and childless marriage. Arthur observed that she "brooded over the fact that she was not essential to anyone."

Yet the morning after the anniversary celebrations, Daisy rose early. She had plans to leave for a trip to India with a school friend, Mary Gale Carter, and one of her nieces, Beth Parker. Her trunks were packed, and off she went.

CHAPTER TEN
A Life-Changing Luncheon

DURING HER TRIP to Egypt with Mabel, Daisy had befriended a group of British military officers, and some of these men were now stationed in India. They provided the three ladies with a servant during their travels around the country and made sure they were safely escorted from place to place. Daisy even visited the Khyber Pass, an important trade route that links Pakistan and Afghanistan in the Hindu Kush mountain range. Her friend Rudyard Kipling had set his 1888 novel, *The Man Who Would Be King*, in this region of steep mountains and narrow river valleys, and she wanted to see for herself the many tribes and cultures there.

It was an exhilarating trip. But while Daisy and her traveling companions were in India, they came down with the chicken pox and had to be quarantined. It was a serious and highly contagious disease. Luckily, the British officers stepped in and cared for them until they recovered. Daisy wrote home, "My own father and brothers cannot have done more, when I was ill, than these officers!"

Once she had recovered, Daisy took a steamer ship to England and returned to her home on Grosvenor Square. A stack of bills must have awaited her, for she was convinced that she was bankrupt. She huddled in bed with her checkbook, trying to figure out her finances. Bills always confused her, and she had a reputation for quarreling with shop owners and tradespeople, sure that she didn't owe them any money when she truly did.

Everyone knew that Daisy was incapable of making and keeping a budget. She hadn't managed her allowance as a schoolgirl, and she still couldn't manage her money. Her accounting system consisted of four envelopes. They were marked "This Year," "Next Year," "Sometime," and "Never."

Papa and Arthur tried to help. They assured her that she had enough money as long as she paid her bills on time, and they made this suggestion: "Wait to get your income before you spend it." One time, Daisy's father was so exasperated, he wrote, "You are not only making an illegal demand for something to which you are not entitled, but you make yourself ridiculous in doing so." He added, "I do hope, for your own sake as well as for the peace of mind of your relatives and business representatives, that you will reform. Your loving Papa." Despite their efforts, Arthur and Papa were never able to change Daisy's ways.

She continued to entertain in England and quietly consulted doctors about her deafness. Her hearing seemed better some days than others, and she was fond of saying, "It comes and goes like the fog." She tried a variety of hearing devices, as they were called then, with little success. She even used one of the first electric hearing aids. "It was a tricky device," according to her nephew Arthur Gordon, "because, if the earpiece got too close to the transmitter, it squealed like an anguished pig." Daisy could not hear the high-pitched sound, but it hurt everyone else's ears.

By then, Daisy was a mature woman in her forties with iron-gray hair. Her nephew Arthur said that she still had her "warm brown eyes, a strong nose, firm mouth, and a *very* determined chin." And she had a beautiful smile. Her face lit up whenever she entered a room full of people, even though it frustrated her not to be able to hear everything they said.

In early 1909, Papa wrote Daisy that William Howard Taft, the twenty-seventh president of the United States, was coming to Savannah in May and would stay overnight in their house. Papa and Taft were acquainted because they had both attended Yale University. Papa asked Daisy for advice about how he and her mother should prepare for the big event. After all, she had successfully entertained the future king of England.

The first electric hearing aids were developed around 1900. Carbon microphones amplified the sound. Patented by Thomas Edison, the carbon microphone was also a key component of Alexander Graham Bell's invention, the telephone. *Hearing Aid Museum/ www.hearingaidmuseum.com*

Daisy suggested that her parents find out about the proper customs and ceremonies when entertaining an American president. Additionally, she thought that her parents should redecorate the house from top to bottom, with fresh paint and new curtains. And she recommended that they hang a big U.S. flag over the front porch.

Mamma took Daisy's advice, even though she grumbled about the expense. Eventually, the Gordon house sparkled inside and out. Bouquets of flowers decorated every room. Even the dining room chairs had been replaced.

Mamma wrote Daisy that the president had arrived in time for a light supper. One of the Gordons' granddaughters sat next to him. She plucked a yellow chrysanthemum from a centerpiece on the table and poked it into the president's lapel as a boutonniere. He was delighted! They chatted while President Taft, a very big man, ate two helpings of everything. He proudly wore his yellow flower at a banquet in Savannah later that evening.

The next morning, the president joined the family for a large, leisurely breakfast that featured Mrs. Gordon's famous waffles buried in butter and maple syrup. Before leaving for a parade downtown, President Taft wrote in the guest book, "With delightful recollections of Savannah hospitality and with the hope of returning when this real commander in chief is in the party." He was referring to his hostess, Nellie Gordon, and the Republican party.

Daisy's parents were in their seventies but still busy and in good health. Since 1906, Daisy had been spending her winters in the United States, which included visits to Savannah. She especially liked to spend time with her father. Together, they rode horses to Papa's farm, Belmont, which was located outside the city, so he could inspect the property, watch his field hands at work, and see how high the cotton was. An Irish terrier named Mr. Dooley often followed them.

Whenever Daisy returned to England, Papa tried to entice her to come back to Savannah by telling her stories about Mr. Dooley or her mother, which he knew

In front of the Gordon home, President Taft sits in the back seat of his touring car following his overnight stay. His automobile, like many in the first decade of the twentieth century, had no top. It was a grand-size vehicle for the times, with four doors and seating to accommodate six to eight people in comfort.
Girl Scouts of the USA-JGLB

she enjoyed. In one letter, Papa joked that Mamma was dashing off her usual thirty letters a day each morning "while brushing her teeth and putting up her back hair." He shared seasonal farm details about the corn, oats, and cotton crops. Because Daisy liked birds, he told her about mockingbird nests around the house and coveys of quail in the fields.

Daisy cherished Papa's love and steadiness. Yet she remained as restless as ever, traveling to Canada and Egypt. Next, she toured Spain and France and wrote home, "I find friends everywhere."

The family hoped that Daisy would settle down and maybe even remarry. Several eligible men did show romantic interest in her, including a few British military officers. One even professed his love. But Daisy felt it wasn't the right time to begin a new relationship. She told her mother, "I am just an idle woman of the world, with no work or duties. I would like to get away . . . and work at sculpturing—start to do some work in life."

In 1911, she wrote this verse, titled "The Road," in her journal, reflecting on some of the unhappiness she had experienced:

The road which led from you to me
Is choked with thorns and overgrown.
We walked together yesterday,
But now—I walk alone.

Finally, Daisy signed up for sculpting lessons in Paris. From the beginning, she loved "modeling," as she called it. She pinched, rolled, and twisted clay into figures, happily working for eight hours a day. Eventually, her teacher told her that she was ready to move forward with sculpting on her own.

Daisy was a talented artist. She could paint in oils or in watercolor, decorate delicate dessert plates with wildlife scenes, forge an iron gate, design clothes, and now work in clay. She enjoyed woodworking, too, and skillfully carved designs onto mahogany dressers and bed frames. Daisy promised her sculpting teacher that she would continue her work at home in her leisure hours, but instead, off she whirled to another party or luncheon. As her brother Arthur would later reflect, "Much of her work reveals real power, which could have been developed had she concentrated upon any one medium."

This painting of Daisy by her niece, Alice Parker Hoyt Shurtleff, now hangs in Daisy's bedroom at the Juliette Gordon Low Birthplace House in Savannah. *Girl Scouts of the USA-JGLB*

At a luncheon in London on May 11, 1911, Daisy sat next to General Sir Robert Baden-Powell, who was known all over Great Britain for his leadership and bravery in the Boer War, a turn-of-the-century power struggle between the British and the Boer people (Dutch immigrants) in South Africa. Daisy had attended hundreds of luncheons like that one, but meeting him was a life-changing experience for her.

A gentle and charming man, Baden-Powell told Daisy about how he had run an experimental camp for teenage boys on Brownsea Island, off the southern coast of Great Britain, while he was in the army. The campers learned first aid and other useful outdoor skills, as well as how to be honest and fair young men. He explained to Daisy that he had gone on to start organized Boy Scouting, which had officially begun in 1908 with the opening of an office in London. The group was growing quickly and spreading outside Great Britain. These stories of his work with the Boy Scouts fascinated Daisy.

She had just returned from her sculpting class and told the general all about it. To her delight, Baden-Powell revealed that he too was a sculptor, as well as an artist in other mediums. They soon discovered that they shared a common ancestor, Captain John Smith, an Englishman who helped establish the colony of Jamestown, in what is now Virginia.

Like Daisy's grandfather and great-grandfather on her mother's side of the family, Baden-Powell had first learned wilderness survival skills in America. He had later used these skills as a soldier, and eventually they spurred the formation of the Boy Scouts. Daisy couldn't wait to tell her mother.

Baden-Powell told Daisy that as a child, he had accompanied his mother on nature walks, where he learned about plants and animals. He had taught himself how to snare a rabbit and cook it. While he was at school at Charterhouse in Godalming, England, he spent a great deal of time in the woods on his own. Tracking animals, leaping streams, and passing through the wilderness without leaving any footprints were other skills he honed as a boy and then used as a soldier. As he rose up the ranks in the army, he trained his men to be equally self-sufficient.

Daisy shared with him the true story of her own great-grandmother's capture by Indians and of her mother's work to revise Ganny Kinzie's book *Wau-Bun, The "Early-Day" in the North-West.*

Within a week, Daisy and Sir Robert Baden-Powell met again, and like his friends and family, she was soon calling him B-P. He often wore a broad-brimmed hat and a handkerchief at his neck, and he carried a walking stick that he had used to leap across streams and wade through swamps in his younger days. The stick was also marked off in centimeters so it could be used for measurement.

On May 30, 1911, Daisy wrote in her journal, "The impression he makes on one is equally contradictory. For instance, all of his portraits and all of his writings represent him in action, essentially a man of war, though never has *any* human being given me such a feeling of peace." Just two days later, she reflected, "A sort of intuition comes over me that [B-P] believes I might make more out of my life, and that he has *ideas* which, if I follow them, will open a more useful sphere of work before me in the future."

B-P was enchanted with Daisy, and he wrote her several notes. In one, he asked her to tea with his mother and sister at the London home they shared. Daisy reciprocated, inviting him to join her in her box seats at the opera.

After discovering another common interest in castles, they motored to the

General Sir Robert Baden-Powell was a military hero in Britain. He built on his childhood and army experiences to found the Boy Scout organization.
Scout Association Trustees

countryside to explore several together. Daisy owned an early model automobile produced by the Ford Motor Company, which had been founded by Henry Ford in 1903. Cars were growing in popularity, and they shared the roads with horse-drawn wagons, bicyclists, riders on horses, pedestrians, and even grazing animals. At the time, drivers were not required to take written or behind-the-wheel exams in Great Britain or the United States. Daisy was a notoriously bad driver.

Billow and his friends hadn't been very interested in intellectual or artistic pursuits. Now Daisy happily chatted with B-P about working in clay and other mediums, and she looked through his sketchbooks.

Their friendship flourished, even though they were both extremely busy. Young men were bombarding Robert Baden-Powell with letters, asking how they could join the Boy Scouts. B-P had published a training manual for soldiers called *Aids to Scouting* in 1905, but he revised it for young scouts. It was renamed *Scouting for*

Daisy (right) enjoys a picnic with B-P and some friends in the rugged Scottish countryside. *Girl Scouts of the USA-NHPC*

Boys and released in 1908. The response was phenomenal. Scout patrols everywhere were influenced by B-P's popular book.

On June 17, Daisy wrote about another meeting with B-P in her journal:

No doubt about his magnetism. I told him a little about my futile efforts to be of use, and the shame I feel when I think of how much I could do, yet how little I accomplish. . . . A wasted life. He looked so kindly when he said, "There are little stars that guide us on, although we do not realize it."

Daisy wondered just when her "little stars" would finally appear.

CHAPTER ELEVEN

An Idea for All of America

ON JUNE 22, 1911, Daisy attended the coronation of King George V. He succeeded Billow's dear friend King Edward VII, who had died a year earlier of a bronchitis-induced heart attack. Edward had been excessively overweight and had smoked cigars and cigarettes for years, which contributed to his poor health. Thousands of people filled the streets of London to see the newly crowned king and his queen, Mary, but they cheered the loudest at the sight of General Baden-Powell, who participated in the ceremony.

Daisy often invited B-P to accompany her on outings and to events, but he was so popular that he was often already booked. Finally, he was able to join her and some friends in Scotland at Lochs. They fished for trout in the streams, and at night, they listened to records on Daisy's Victrola, which had been a present from Mamma. Over and over again, she had thanked her mother for the wonderful gift. As they listened to recordings of operas that they had both seen in London, Daisy saw yet another side of

This is a Victor Talking Machine, similar to a Victrola, one of the earliest record players. Daisy loved to listen to records and play them as loudly as she wished. *Author's collection*

B-P. He liked to pretend to sing the various songs and act out scenes with Daisy and her guests.

During his stay, B-P also shared his evolving plans for the Boy Scouts. In 1909, he had invited all the scouts to meet him for a rally at the Crystal Palace in London, an exposition hall made of cast iron and glass. Eleven thousand Boy Scouts showed up, and he was stunned. Much to Baden-Powell's surprise, thousands of English *girls* had signed up to attend the rally too. He realized that there was much he could offer to the growing group, so he resigned from the army to devote all his time to the Boy Scout organization. Even King Edward VII had encouraged B-P to work full-time for the movement.

From Scotland, Daisy wrote Papa:

The Girl Guides is a sort of outcome of the Boy Scouts. When Baden-Powell first formed the Boy Scouts, six thousand girls registered as Scouts. And as he could not have girls traipsing about over the country after his Boy Scouts, he got his sister, Miss Agnes Baden-Powell, to form a society of Girl Guides [in 1910]. . . . I like girls and I like the organization and the rules and pastimes, so if you find that I get very deeply interested you must not be surprised.

Girl Guides was based on B-P's scouting principles for boys. The organization's first president, Agnes Baden-Powell, declared, "Girls must be partners and comrades, rather than dolls." Agnes had many interests, from astronomy to art to natural history. She also participated in sports such as skating and swimming, played musical instruments, was skilled in nursing, and kept bees, birds, and butterflies in her home. And she knew eleven languages! It was no surprise that Agnes and Daisy enjoyed each other's company.

B-P was a thoughtful man. He knew that Daisy desperately needed to find herself and do something meaningful with her life. Yet he suggested that she not rush into getting involved with Girl Guides unless it truly appealed to her. Perhaps he was aware of her tendency to throw herself into a new hobby only to later lose interest.

This time, Daisy wasn't about to get sidetracked. She *really* liked the basic principles of Girl Guides. Girls and young women would develop self-esteem and confidence, leadership skills, healthy lifestyles, and friendships around the world and also reach out to others as part of a team, all while experiencing a sense of adventure.

Headstrong as ever, Daisy told her father in August 1911, "I am getting up a corp[s] of Girl Guides here in this glen where the Highland Girls are so far from the world they remain ignorant of all details of nursing the sick and the way to feed and bring up delicate children."

She had already dashed off handwritten invitations to every girl in her area to come to tea. On a Saturday afternoon, seven nervous farm girls were ushered into Daisy's home. They all lived in Glen Lyon's long, narrow valley, their remote cottages scattered far apart. One girl walked six miles to reach Daisy's house.

Agnes Baden-Powell, the first president of Girl Guides and the sister of Robert Baden-Powell, founder of Boy Scouts. *Girl Scouts of the USA–JGLB*

Along with tea, Daisy offered her guests warm scones, bread and butter, strawberry jam, and cakes. The just-baked delicacies were served on fragile dishes hand-painted by Daisy and her sisters, and accompanied by white linen napkins. While enjoying the delicious food, the fire in the fireplace, and the promise of friendship, the girls listened to Daisy discuss Girl Guides, captivated by her lively, inviting personality.

They returned to Daisy's home every Saturday during that summer of 1911. Daisy made it a rule that each meeting should include tea. In the early meetings, the new Girl Guides studied the history of the British flag and how to tie knots. With the help of some handsome young Scots Guards officers staying in nearby Meggernie Castle, they were taught other skills that the Boy Scouts were also mastering, such as map reading and signaling with flags. The girls also learned first aid and personal hygiene, starting with the importance of brushing one's teeth.

All the girls in Daisy's group came from poor rural families, and it distressed her that they and their brothers were expected to eventually move to the big cities to work in factories. At the time, factory owners often hired children and women because they were desperate enough to work longer hours than most men, and for lower wages. There were few government regulations to protect them from what were often unsafe and unhealthy work sites. Living conditions for those who toiled in the factories were also crowded and unsanitary, and it was not uncommon for the workers to contract diseases like tuberculosis and die young.

Daisy was determined to keep *her* girls in Glen Lyon by teaching them usable domestic skills and introducing career ideas. The land was rocky, with poor soil, so it was hard to grow much of anything. Flocks of sheep grazed on whatever they could find in the valley. Daisy taught herself how to card and spin the raw wool on a spinning wheel, and she shared her knowledge with her Girl Guides. She even located a shop in London that promised to buy the yarn. As fall and winter approached, the girls had to spin the wool in the dark, because their families couldn't afford to burn extra candles for light.

Daisy also encouraged her girls to raise the healthiest, and therefore the best-producing and tastiest, chickens in the glen. Although there is no written record of it, she apparently found a farmer who taught them all about the birds. In the autumn, when the local lodges filled with hunters, Daisy's Girl Guides supplied them with chickens and eggs.

All too soon, it was time for Daisy to return to her home in London for the winter. She surprised the village's postmistress by asking her to take charge of her patrol of Girl Guides while she was away. The postmistress agreed.

Daisy at her spinning wheel in Scotland. *Girl Scouts of the USA-JGLB*

In London, Daisy again signed up for sculpting classes at night, and she filled her calendar with social events. But her energies were still centered on the Girl Guides, and she started two new patrols there, including one in Lambeth, a poor and dangerous part of the city.

Then the ever-restless Daisy prepared to sail to America. She asked some adult committee members of the Girl Guides in London to continue working with the main group there. Daisy then told Rose Kerr, another volunteer whom she knew only slightly, to take charge of the second patrol of girls in Lambeth.

Mrs. Kerr protested, saying that she didn't have the time and wasn't really good with girls. She recalled how Daisy responded: "'Then that is settled,' she said serenely, turning her deaf ear to me. 'The next meeting is on Thursday and I have told them you will take it.'"

Daisy promised to pay the expenses for the Lambeth girls, and as she was leaving, she added, "And I should like you to give them a good tea every week after the meeting. Good-bye."

Scottish Girl Guides learning how to light a fire. *Girl Scouts of the USA-JGLB*

Despite Daisy's abrupt departure, she and Rose Kerr became friends over the years. And as Rose learned, she was just one of many acquaintances and friends who encountered what she described as Daisy's "genius for not hearing any excuses or refusal or, in fact, anything she did not want to hear. She simply smiled at you—and what a smile was hers—and said, 'Here are the girls. You will start at once.'"

On January 6, 1912, Daisy set sail for New York on the ocean liner SS *Arcadian*. It was going from London to the West Indies and then on to New York. General Sir Baden-Powell was onboard too, for the start of his world tour to visit the Boy Scouts in America and elsewhere. Daisy and B-P talked about how she might sow "the seeds of the Girl Guide movement in her own country for the first time."

While onboard, Daisy met the other first-class passengers, including Miss Olave Soames, a young woman who was traveling with her father to the West Indies. Olave was drawn to Daisy, recalling, "There was something magnetic about her, so clever and so witty she was. Interested in herself and interested too in other people, full of enthusiasms and with vision and vigour, determined at this moment to start guides in her own home land."

Miss Soames and B-P fell in love during the brief sea journey, even though Olave was just twenty-three and B-P was fifty-five. They became secretly engaged. Olave left the ship in the West Indies with her father, but she later reminisced about that romantic voyage: "There we met on board ship, there we fell in love, and there we decided to marry."

Later, many friends and family, including Olave Baden-Powell, would repeat the story that B-P had once proposed marriage to Daisy and she had turned him down, saying that he should have children. Despite the refusal, they formed a life-long friendship.

Following her sea voyage on the SS *Arcadian*, Daisy visited friends in New York and New Jersey before boarding a train for Savannah. As the train chugged south and crossed the Savannah River, Daisy finally spotted the familiar Georgia fields where cotton would be planted later in the spring. There were forests of pine trees, live oaks, and palmetto palms. She had crossed the Atlantic Ocean between Great Britain and New York many times and had taken the train up and down the East Coast, but her eagerness to introduce Girl Guides to her country made this particular trip seem to take forever.

Robert and Olave Baden-Powell shortly after their marriage. The car was a wedding gift from the Boy Scout organization in Great Britain. *Scout Association Trustees*

She recalled the wonderful summers of her childhood, playing with all her cousins along Georgia's Etowah River, hiking, swimming, and trapping fireflies in jars. Before long, all of America's girls would have the opportunity to have as much fun as she and her cousins had so long ago. It was all part of her plan.

Years later, Rose Kerr wrote about how she envisioned Daisy's arrival in Savannah that spring. "Imagine a woman, delicate, no longer young [and] handicapped by deafness, deliberately setting out to conquer the United States for Girl Guiding! Had she been a woman to be daunted by difficulties, she would have thrown it all to the winds."

As Mrs. Kerr clearly understood, Daisy did not feel daunted or handicapped. She felt exhilarated with anticipation as she stepped off the train. A porter loaded her many trunks and belongings into a large car, and Daisy climbed in after them, with her Pekingese named Chi-chi in her arms. According to her nephew Arthur, the dog was "a moth-eaten specimen . . . whose back legs were so much longer than those in front. . . . Daisy loved him." Polly Poons squawked in her cage as the car began to clatter over cobblestone streets.

Leaning out the window, Daisy saw the city's familiar squares decorated with fountains, statues, and ancient oaks draped in Spanish moss. Dogwood trees and azaleas were in full bloom. It was early March, and all of Savannah was awash in color.

Whenever she returned to Savannah, Daisy arrived at this train station with her trunks and pets. *Georgia Historical Society*

Daisy settled into her parents' home at 10 East Oglethorpe because she had rented out her house. She was eager to update her family and friends about everything she had been doing in Great Britain. Daisy had written home about her new dreams and direction in life, but it would be so much easier to explain everything in person!

One day not long after her arrival in Savannah, she called her cousin, Nina Anderson Pape. "Come right over," she shouted into the telephone. "I've got something for the girls of Savannah and all America and all the world, and we're going to start it tonight!"

CHAPTER TWELVE

Launching a Dream

NINA WAS EAGER to find out what unusual idea her beloved cousin had this time. Knowing Daisy, it was sure to be a doozy!

That evening, Daisy's brown eyes sparkled, and Nina thought she looked more relaxed than ever. Daisy shared the story of her first meeting with General Sir Robert Baden-Powell at the luncheon and how they discovered many common interests, from sculpture to their love of young people, even though neither of them had children of their own.

Nina learned from Daisy that B-P had started an organization in England called the Boy Scouts. And Daisy also told her about meeting his sister, Agnes, who had started the Girl Guides. Thousands of young girls had already joined.

Daisy was wildly enthusiastic about the success of the three patrols she had started in Great Britain, and now she was back in Savannah, ready to bring Girl Guides to all of America. Because Nina was a school principal, Daisy thought she might have some valuable suggestions. Daisy explained that as Girl Guides, the girls would learn self-reliance and skills that would help them be successful adults both during their careers and at home as parents. In addition to honing their domestic abilities, the activities would expose the girls to other useful knowledge, such as first aid. And they would encourage the girls to be physically fit.

In 1912, many women of Daisy's social status lived a restricted life. Daisy intended to break down those walls of tradition. She wanted the upcoming generations of girls to grow with the changing world—where some women were getting involved in local and national elections, going to college, and even seeking careers outside the home. Daisy believed that they could and should do anything they wished!

Nina hoped that the organization would give Daisy something meaningful to do. She mentioned a group of Savannah girls who belonged to a nature-oriented camp. They met every Saturday at Bona Bella Woods, just outside the city, to learn about plants and animals and to cook their supper over a campfire. The program was run by W. J. Hoxie, a naturalist and a retired military officer. Nina thought maybe some of these young women would want to be Girl Guides as well.

On March 2, 1912, Daisy wrote to Mamma, who was in Chicago. She bragged about an article

Nina Anderson Pape was Daisy's cousin and the principal at a local girls' school.
Girl Scouts of the USA–JGLB

she had written for the *Savannah Morning News* about why young women should join Girl Guides, saying, "I may become a literary genius if you remain away much longer." After her mother's return, Daisy recruited her and ten friends to be on the first board of Girl Guides in America. She also told her sister Mabel that she was creating a new handbook for American girls. She asked the naturalist W. J. Hoxie to write the sections that were inspired by his outdoor program in Savannah, and with Agnes Baden-Powell's permission, she adapted parts of the English handbook for Girl Guides. "I am deep in Girl Guides," she wrote to Mabel. "You must not be bored with G.G.s as I can't write of anything else."

Shortly after her meeting with the board members, Daisy invited some local girls, including those suggested by Nina, to a tea party at her mother's house. Mrs. Gordon, as spry and tart-tongued as ever, later commented that her daughter served a tea that was fancy enough for the president of the United States. Daisy showed her young guests pictures of busy Girl Guides in England, shared with them the existing official handbook, and discussed the badges they could earn for mastering skills such as knot tying or nature studies. By the end of the afternoon, the girls were eager to join and excitedly chatting among themselves about what their uniforms should look like.

There are several different versions of what happened in Savannah on March 12, 1912, the historic day when Daisy held her first official Girl Guide meeting at the Louisa Porter Home in Savannah. We know that seventeen girls signed up that day and were divided into two groups, the White Rose patrol and the Carnation patrol. At the top of the register, Daisy wrote the name of her twelve-year-old niece and namesake, Margaret Eleanor "Daisy Doots" Gordon, even though she was twenty-three miles away at Myrtle Beach Plantation in Richmond Hill with her family at the time.

Daisy selected two mothers to be the adult leaders of the patrols and, before anyone could protest, handed over her copy of the English handbook to one of them. She smiled. "Here are the girls. You will start at once." As Rose Kerr noted, in the years to come, these two simple and much-repeated sentences would become familiar, and sometimes feared, by other women Daisy selected to help the organization.

Doots would later write about her Aunt Daisy's surprise visit to the plantation after the first Girl Guides meeting, in *Lady from Savannah: The Life of Juliette Low.*

> *"You've made me a what?" Doots asked.*
>
> *"A Girl Guide. All the girls in Savannah are going to be Girl Guides."*
>
> *"Why?"*
>
> *"Because it is a wonderful thing to be," Daisy replied.*
>
> *"How did you make me into a Guide?"*
>
> *"I put your name down." Daisy was beginning to be impatient.*

Daisy listed what the girls in Savannah would be doing together: cooking, learning first aid, taking nature hikes, wearing uniforms, and earning badges. Doots had no choice but to agree with her strong-willed aunt. After all, she had already "joined," thanks to Daisy. Because her name topped the official March 12 list, Margaret Eleanor "Daisy Doots" Gordon became the first Girl Guide in America. When the name of the organization was changed to Girl Scouts in 1913, the Girl Scouts in the USA claimed her as the first Girl Scout as well. It was an honor Doots later cherished.

During her visit with her brother and his family that spring, Daisy also created a sculpture of her niece's head. Doots recalled "sitting perched on a high stool for hours and hours each day while Aunt Daisy, completely absorbed in shaping the moist clay, even forgot meals." When the sculpture was completed, Daisy dashed back to Savannah.

Within a few short weeks, some sixty Savannah girls belonged to Girl Guides. Soon, women from other cities were contacting Daisy for information about how to start their own groups. There was no doubt in her mind that with hard work, Girl Guides would soon spread across the country. It was just the beginning, and Daisy was elated!

The girls designed their own uniform patterns, selected the fabric, and pinned, cut, and sewed them. They wore blouses with sailor-style collars, knee-length skirts

Unlike today's female athletes who wear lightweight shorts and tops, women and girls in the early twentieth century were expected to be fully covered by clothing while playing sports or enjoying outdoor activities, as this photograph of a 1913 Savannah Girl Scout basketball team shows. *Girl Scouts of the USA–JGLB*

SAVANNAH GIRL SCOUTS

HEADQUARTERS
330 DRAYTON STREET
TELEPHONE 7315
SAVANNAH, GEORGIA
1912 - 1937

On March 12th, 1912, Juliette Low held the first meeting of Girl Guides in order to organize the movement in this country.

We testify that we were present at the Louisa Porter Home in Savannah, Georgia where the meeting was held, and that we officially registered our names as the charter members of the Girl Guides (now the Girl Scouts) of the United States. This group was divided into two patrols. The White Rose and The Carnation.

WHITE ROSE	CARNATION
Martha Randolph Stevens	Daisy Gordon Lawrence
Anne Read Charlton	Elizabeth Sheele Klein
Eleanor Taylor Faine	Berenice Fetzer Almutt
Jean Cunningham Reade	Nannie Bleward Rowland S.
Page R. Anderson Platt	Elizabeth Powell
Cecilia Pansard	Elsie Espy Frank
Louisa Gaines Lambert	Marian Corbin Aslakson
Helen Brigham Radebusch	Florence Gane Norvell
	Gertrude Porter Driscoll
	Walton Brewer Henry

*Daisy Gordon was not present at this meeting, but was previously enrolled as the first Girl Scout by Juliette Low.

This 1936 document contains the signatures of the girls who officially registered their names as Girl Guides (now Girl Scouts) on March 12, 1912. *Girl Scouts of the USA-NHPC*

of heavy dark blue cotton twill, and light blue sateen ties. Large black hair ribbons and long black stockings rounded out the ensemble.

The Girl Guides also traced a trefoil, a three-lobed leaf, onto felt and cut it out to make a Tenderfoot badge. This badge signified a girl who was just starting out and learning about scouting and her individual patrol. Eventually, the word *patrol* was replaced with *troop*. At first, each patrol or troop was named for a flower, shrub, or tree. But decades later, as the organization grew, the troop names were replaced with numbers, such as Troop 695. The number of badges and pins changed over time too. Girl Scout insignia are still made of metal and cloth, as they were in 1912.

That spring was particularly busy for Daisy. Once again, President Taft, along with his daughter, Helen, visited the Gordons from May 1 to May 3, and Daisy was there to help her parents receive them. Her Girl Guides also made their first public appearance in their new uniforms in a May Day festival in a Savannah park, where they performed some English folk dances. They made quite an impression, and soon more girls wanted to join Girl Guides and wear the uniforms.

When she was satisfied that the organization was well established in Savannah, Daisy headed back to England to check on her property. While she was away, the stable and servants' quarters at the back of her rented house on Savannah's Abercorn Street were transformed into the Girl Guide headquarters, where the girls met every Saturday. A vacant lot across the street was used for games.

Miss Edith Johnston, who would become the first national secretary of the Girl Guides in the United States, commented that the girls kept busy while Daisy was gone. "We played games on our vacant lot. We took hikes, especially bird hikes, keeping bird notes and greatly enjoying our nature study. We formed an inter-troop basket-ball league."

The *Savannah Morning News* even printed a weekly column about what the various groups were doing.

Daisy's father rode by the headquarters and wrote his daughter in mid-May: "The rooms were packed with them like a swarm of bees. . . . You are certainly giving a great deal of pleasure to a large number of individuals."

From England, Daisy wrote letters to her new Girl Guides in Savannah. Miss Johnston recalled that they were "filled with quaintly misspelled words" and shared

From this desk, Daisy wrote hundreds of letters to friends and acquaintances, inviting them to help her achieve her dreams and goals for America's young women. The desk could be disassembled and shipped easily, so Daisy may have moved it back and forth between her homes in Savannah and Great Britain. *Girl Scouts of the USA–JGLB*

details about what the English Girl Guides were doing. The Girl Guides was still a young organization there, too, but they had an official headquarters in London. Daisy visited and asked question after question in an effort to find out what was working and what was not. She hoped to apply what she learned to her organization back in the States.

Brimming with information and carrying handfuls of badges, she returned to Savannah. There, Daisy visited every troop. She talked to each of the leaders. "Miss Daisy," as the girls affectionately called her, had found something meaningful to do with her life.

But suddenly, all of Daisy's plans came to a grinding halt. In mid-August, Papa became very ill, and Mamma summoned the family to his bedside. Papa grew sicker and sicker, and on September 11, 1912, he died. William Gordon was buried in Laurel Grove Cemetery near his daughter Alice. In Savannah, flags flew at half-mast in his honor. Letters praising his service to his country, his state, and his community arrived from around the world.

CHAPTER THIRTEEN
The Dream Builds

FOLLOWING GENERAL GORDON'S DEATH, Nellie suffered a breakdown. She talked to her husband as though he had just stepped out to another room. Worried, Daisy stayed at her mother's side night and day. A doctor examined Mrs. Gordon and reported to the family, "Her heart, kidneys, liver, all are absolutely normal. She is simply stunned."

Daisy came up with a plan to take her mother to England. Perhaps being around Mabel, Rowland, and their two young children, Rowland and Peggy, would lift Nellie's spirits. Everyone in the family remembered her long months of melancholy following Alice's death and agreed that the trip might help.

After making sure her mother was settled in at Mabel's, Daisy traveled to Harrogate, a spa town in North Yorkshire, England. She told her friends and family that she needed to soak in the healing mineral waters because her rheumatism had

Being with Mabel's busy family helped Mamma heal after Papa's death. *Girl Scouts of the USA-JGLB*

flared up. But Daisy really needed to mourn her father privately. No one heard from her for weeks, and the family worried. Mabel wrote to say that Mamma was improving, although slowly. Arthur wrote several times too and sent his sister a gift for her fifty-second birthday.

She finally responded to Arthur on December 1, explaining her long silence by saying, "I don't think it helps to write when one is *ill*." Daisy told him she felt that she had "lost, in Papa, the only human being who was indulgent to my faults, and took my part in all ways and always. . . . He loved me not more than the others, but he knew I needed him more, and in proportion I miss him more."

Eventually, both Daisy and her mother climbed out of their deep wells of sadness, and Daisy resumed her busy social schedule. She was still an attractive woman, and several British military officers, including Nevill M. Smyth, whom she had met on her trip to India, called on her in England and escorted her to various events. But Daisy remained committed to the Girl Guides and chose to dedicate her life to "her girls." Nevill spoke to her troops about flying airplanes and, along with B-P and his wife, Olave, advised her on the direction Girl Guides should take in the United States.

When Daisy returned to Savannah, she started making arrangements to purchase some wooded lots near Bona Bella. The girls enjoyed day-camping activities there, such as signaling with flags and learning how to identify animal tracks. Then Daisy bought the Girl Guides a boat to use on the surrounding network of rivers. In addition, they continued to march and play basketball on the property near Daisy's home.

This photo shows some of the early Savannah Girl Scouts shooting basketballs in the lot across the street from Daisy's house. *Girl Scouts of the USA–JGLB*

More and more local girls signed up, as did young women who assisted the troop leaders, including eighteen-year-old Eleanor Nash, who volunteered as a Guide Mistress. Because her parents were renting Daisy's house on Abercorn Street, Eleanor only had to step out the back door to help with meetings in the carriage house or to play on the basketball court.

The Girl Guides in the first White Rose patrol went on a five-day camping trip organized and led by Daisy. It was always fun to spend time with Miss Daisy and enjoy her sense of humor and loud, infectious laugh. They learned camping techniques that the Boy Scouts used and that Daisy's great-grandmother had learned while traveling west in a wagon. The girls swam, cooked outdoors, paddled canoes, and gathered around campfires in the evenings. As one young camper shared, Daisy "could tell ghost stories till your blood ran cold."

They had a great time, and only two complaints. Clouds of biting mosquitoes pestered the campers the entire trip, and the light-colored Georgia soil quickly made their dark blue uniforms look dirty. Eventually, troop leaders decided that it would be more practical to have khaki-colored uniforms that didn't highlight the dirt.

Some of the activities that the Girl Guides participated in were considered radical in 1913. Many people felt that hiking and rigorous sports such as basketball were too strenuous and would make the girls less ladylike. Daisy, who had been raised to be an independent woman, disagreed. She believed in fostering active, healthy, and strong-minded girls who would eventually make their own life choices about marriage, having children, and even careers. Luckily, most families in Savannah respected the Gordons, and they trusted Daisy with their daughters.

Daisy charged forward with the final preparations for her handbook for

America's Girl Guides. *How Girls Can Help Their Country: Handbook for Girl Scouts* was published in 1913. By using "Girl Scouts" in the title, Daisy was clearly separating her organization from the Girl Guides. Part One reads:

> *Girls will do no good by trying to imitate boys. It is better to be a real girl such as no boy can be. . . . Scouting for girls is not the same kind of scouting as for boys. The chief difference is the courses of instruction. . . . For the girls it all tends to WOMANLINESS and enables girls the better to help in the great battle of life.*

In the handbook, Girl Scouts were encouraged to "welcome all obstacles, as it is only by meeting with difficulties that you can know how to overcome them and be prepared for others in the future." Daisy continued to refer to the Girl Guides in the United States as Girl Scouts. Writing an article for the *Savannah Morning News*, she declared, "I selected the name 'Scouts' because the American likes to be original and I knew they would reject the name 'Guides.'" Actually, English girls had called themselves Girl Scouts too in the early months of 1910, just before and after the Crystal Palace rally, until they were organized into the Girl Guides by Agnes Baden-Powell. Even Daisy's English

An early Girl Scout handbook. *Girl Scouts of the USA–JGLB*

friend Rose Kerr used the words "Girl Scouts" in a January 9, 1913, letter to Daisy on Girl Guides letterhead.

By this time, the girls were regularly reciting early versions of today's Girl Scout Promise and Laws at the start of each meeting:

The Girl Scout Promise

On my honor, I will try:
To do my duty to God and to my country,
To help other people at all times,
To Obey the Laws of the Scouts.

The Girl Scout Laws

1. *A Girl Scout's Honor Is to be Trusted*
2. *A Girl Scout Is Loyal*
3. *A Girl Scout's Duty Is to be Useful and to Help Others*
4. *A Girl Scout Is a Friend to All, and a Sister to every Other Girl Scout no Matter to what Social Class she May Belong*
5. *A Girl Scout Is Courteous*
6. *A Girl Scout Keeps herself Pure*
7. *A Girl Scout Is a Friend to Animals*
8. *A Girl Scout Obeys Orders*
9. *A Girl Scout Is Cheerful*
10. *A Girl Scout Is Thrifty*

Daisy had gradually won over those who had privately thought her vision for a national or even a worldwide Girl Scouting movement was a frivolous idea. Slowly, one by one, friends, family, and even strangers began to listen to Daisy Low, and many offered to help. And they encouraged their daughters to join Girl Scouts so they could go camping, learn about animals, expand their knowledge of United States history, study the stars, and take part in additional activities that were not usually available to girls at that time, such as archery, rowing, and other team sports. Daisy also felt strongly about the importance of building "womanly" traits, so there were badges and activities involving home safety, cooking, and caring for babies, to prepare the Girl Scouts to be homemakers and parents. Those close to Daisy were delighted to see her so happy, and everyone admired her boundless energy.

Soon, Daisy decided to open a national headquarters in Washington, D.C. Nell, who lived there with her husband, Wayne Parker, a congressman from New Jersey, helped her find an office. Daisy furnished it and hired a part-time office assistant. Then she convinced her friend Edith Johnston to move to Washington in the fall of 1913 to run the headquarters. Although Edith was reluctant at first, she eventually agreed. "I could not refuse her," she recalled. "I had seen what Girl Guiding had come to mean to our Savannah girls in one short year. I knew what it would mean to girls everywhere if it could be brought to them." Although the name had been changed to Girl Scouts, many of the leaders, including Edith Johnston, would occasionally refer to the organization as Girl Guides and use the word *patrol* instead of *troop*.

After establishing the office, Daisy began telling all her Washington friends about the Girl Scouts. Then off she dashed to New York, Baltimore, Boston, and other large East Coast cities to spread the word. Daisy was a dynamic and skilled speaker, and she captivated her audiences, along with any newspaper reporters who wanted to interview her. And from her office, Edith Johnston did everything she could behind the scenes to make Daisy and her Girl Scouts organization succeed, including answering requests for information, attending meetings, and filling orders for the handbook.

Daisy was in contact with many important people, and she didn't hesitate to reach out and ask for help. In Chicago, she was the guest of Jane Addams, a well-known social reformer. In the early twentieth century, thousands of newly arrived European immigrants needed help finding jobs and learning English in the overcrowded cities. Jane and her friend Ellen Gates Starr had established Hull House in Chicago, a place where immigrant women and children could temporarily settle and make the transition from rural lives in their home countries to urban life in America. There were similar settlement houses, as they were called, in other cities, but Hull House was the most well known. Daisy's organization, which was open to girls of all backgrounds, must have appealed to Jane.

Soon, Nell began pitching in at the national Girl Scout headquarters and enlisted the help of two prominent friends, Corinne Roosevelt Robinson, who was Theodore Roosevelt's sister, and Thomas Edison's wife, Mina. Even Nellie Gordon, still spunky and outspoken despite two heart attacks following Willie's death, worked at the headquarters. She told Mabel that she didn't "give a [damn] about the Girl Scouts and Eleanor doesn't either. We are so glad Daisy is sticking to her interest that we want to do everything we can." Daisy's life finally had purpose. Mabel commented that her sister would butt her head against a brick wall and smash it to pieces to accomplish her goals. But now the head bashing wasn't to serve her own interests, but for the girls.

Only one thing came before Girl Scouts for Daisy, and that was Mamma. At the age of seventy-nine, she was just as Rudyard Kipling had once described her in one of his magazine stories: "a little old lady with snapping black eyes, who used very bad language." In 1914, Daisy rented Castle Menzies in Scotland and invited Mamma and the rest of the family to come for the summer. "Everything is done up new . . . and . . . it all does look nice," Daisy wrote on June 22, after moving her furniture from London into the castle.

By the end of July, Mamma, Nell and her children Beth and Corty, and Mabel and her son, Rowland, had all arrived. Daisy was delighted to discover that her castle came with a ghost, and she told Arthur in a letter, "Mam[m]a says she *likes* my haunted castle."

But their quiet days in Scotland were soon over. Germany declared war on Russia on August 1, and on France on August 3. The next day, Germany invaded the neutral country of Belgium. As a result, Great Britain declared war on Germany. By August 6, Austria-Hungary had allied with Germany. Europe was thrown into turmoil.

Castle Menzies in Perthshire, Scotland, where Daisy lived for part of 1914.
Iain Struthers Photography

The assassination of Archduke Francis Ferdinand, the heir apparent to the Austro-Hungarian throne, and his wife on June 28, 1914, had ignited the tensions. Now the fighting had spread and was disrupting trade routes, causing shortages of food and other supplies. President Woodrow Wilson called upon the United States to remain neutral and promised a safe passage home for stranded citizens in England.

Daisy managed to stock up on food before it became scarce, and she purchased an oil stove in case they couldn't get enough coal. There wasn't much gasoline available for nonmilitary vehicles, and Daisy's horses were commandeered by the armed services for transportation. She decided that she would bicycle to nearby farms to purchase local produce or stay safely inside to work on her sculpting.

Nell had left for the United States before Great Britain entered the war. Finally, in the fall, Mamma sailed home on a troopship with Beth and Corty. Mabel and Rowland returned to their home in England, and Daisy went to London in December. The Great War, or the War to End All Wars, as many people called it, escalated until it involved most of the powerful countries of Europe. Many decades later, it would come to be known as World War I.

Despite the wartime conditions, Daisy was able to return to the United States in January 1915. For a few months, she busied herself by keeping the national Girl Scouts headquarters running, and she personally paid for all uniforms, the printing of the handbook, and Girl Scouting–related government patents. The organization named Daisy their first president and held their first annual convention.

Because of the war, Daisy couldn't access all her money, since it was tied up in English property and securities. She still had some resources, but she tried to go without. "I must save every penny for my Girl Scouts and no lights may go on until half-past five!" she wrote. She saw to it that nothing was thrown out in the kitchen, and guests were served leftovers.

On May 1, 1915, a passenger vessel called the *Lusitania* left New York for Liverpool, England. Six days later, as it neared the coast of Ireland, a German submarine attacked and sank it. Among the 1,198 people who died were 128 U.S. citizens.

Americans were incensed, and many called on President Wilson to declare war on Germany. The president refused to be drawn into the growing European conflict but asserted that U.S. citizens had the right to travel at sea. Nonetheless, floating and sub-

Daisy desperately needed cash to support the growing Girl Scout organization, so she sold a fabulous pearl necklace similar to the one she's wearing in this photograph. *Girl Scouts of the USA-JGLB*

merged mines in the ocean and a German fleet that intended to torpedo boats carrying supplies made travel between the United States and Europe dangerous. Despite this, Daisy sailed to Liverpool that June, following her mother's eightieth birthday. The fate of the *Lusitania* was on everyone's mind.

It was just as dangerous on land. Friends in Britain sent Daisy letters describing loved ones who had been injured, were missing in action, or had died. She had

After being struck by a German torpedo, the *Lusitania* sank in eighteen minutes. *Bundes Archive*

watched many of these young men grow up. She shared the awful news with her immediate family, and together they cried over the cruelty of war.

Daisy penned many letters of condolence. According to her brother Arthur, she was quite religious and read the Bible frequently, and these sad letters were often accompanied by well-known biblical quotations. One of the most difficult letters for her to write was addressed to her friends Rudyard and Carrie Kipling on the death of their son, John, in 1915.

CHAPTER FOURTEEN

The Organization Grows

DAISY'S BRITISH FRIENDS AND FAMILY closely followed the news of the major battles in Europe. Tens of thousands of soldiers were injured or killed. Those not in active military service volunteered in their towns and cities, ready and willing to pitch in where they were needed. To do her share, Daisy continued working with her Girl Guides and their leaders. She helped set up training for three hundred Girl Guides in cooking and first aid, so they could provide support to soldiers and their families.

The *Savannah Morning News* reported on May 7, 1916, that Girl Guides in London were helping with the war effort by delivering messages around the city on bicycles, and cooking food for workers in ammunition factories. They were "rushing through factories daily, basket on arm, to serve it."

Daisy considered going to Belgium to participate in a new relief program started in late 1914 by an American couple, Herbert and Lou Henry Hoover. The program helped Belgian families who were left without food or homes after the German invasion. But when the Germans executed Edith Cavell, an English nurse, in Belgium on October 12, 1915, Daisy rethought her plans. Instead, she and Mabel became active in the Belgian war relief efforts in London.

As the war continued, Mabel decided to forego her biannual visits to America and stay in England with her British husband and their children. But Daisy sailed back and forth between England and the United States several times. Once, she accompanied her eighty-one-year-old mother to England because Mamma wanted to see Mabel and her family.

While the Gordons were separated from Mabel, they could still send letters and telegrams. Mamma wrote proudly, "Daisy's Scouts are booming! [And] she is doing many wonderful *stunts* for them."

Dashing about on behalf of Girl Scouts or Girl Guides, Daisy, who had never been punctual, seldom arrived in Savannah, New York, London, or any place on time. Her plans were always changing, and often no one in the family was sure exactly where she was. As Mamma wrote to Mabel, "I do not know how she lives through it all—losing things every hour—telephoning every minute—changing her plans every second!" Daisy even lost her passport more than once.

Daisy wrote Mabel too, noting gleefully that their mother, in one of her letters, had put two *l*'s in the word *balance*. She went on to say that she had written back, "I never use the word myself as I have not a balance anywhere, either in my actions or in my bank."

Daisy's spelling was as bad as ever, of course. In one letter, she wrote, "I want to arrive by the eighteenth but this octobus [octopus?] movement of Girl Scouts is growing by leaps and bounds." She sometimes even misspelled her proper first name, Juliette. Mamma and everyone else did their best to interpret Daisy's spelling and learned not to expect her until they actually saw her.

Daisy's driving continued to be just as awful as her spelling. Only a few states had initiated laws requiring written and behind-the-wheel tests for drivers. Georgia had no such exams. Daisy kept a car in Savannah, and she still had very limited knowledge about her "motor." But she didn't let that stop her from enjoying automobile outings.

When she was ready to leave for the day, she had a servant back the car out of the driveway and point it in the right direction. Her cook and butler would stop traffic as Daisy started up the engine, a process that was usually accompanied by loud backfiring. Then the car might lurch forward as Daisy headed down the road on the wrong side of the street, often waving enthusiastically to her terrified neighbors.

Once, Daisy drove her motor through the wall of a house, coming to a stop in the dining room while the family inside was eating a meal. She backed out and later called her brother Bill to explain what happened. She told Bill that she didn't talk to the people in the house because she "didn't think it would be polite to bother them while they were eating!" The citizens of Savannah and Great Britain quickly learned to get out of Daisy's way when she was on the road, and, miraculously, no one was ever hurt.

Around this time, Daisy hired Bella MacDonald, a Scottish woman who would become a trusted maid and take care of Daisy for the rest of her life. Bella seemed to understand "Miss Daisy." If a group of women showed up for lunch and Daisy had

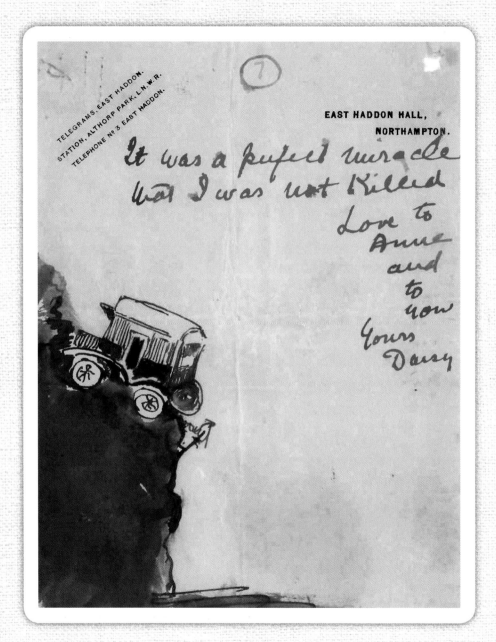

Daisy drew this picture to illustrate one of her driving mishaps. Her friend Rudyard Kipling commented, "She had ways of her own in driving her Ford in Scotland that chilled my blood and even impressed our daughter. But her own good angels looked after her even when she was on one wheel over a precipice." *Girl Scouts of the USA-JGLB*

forgotten the date and wasn't around, Bella always invited them in and prepared an elegant meal.

Despite missing luncheons and trains, Daisy forged ahead with her dreams of expanding the Girl Scout organization, determined to encourage all of America's young girls to get an education, experience a career, *and* enjoy a family, if they wanted. The organization was growing and changing constantly.

In 1915, Daisy approached her goddaughter, Anne Hyde Choate, and asked her to become involved in Girl Scouts. Anne, who lived in New York, thought she would "just pin on badges once a year." But before she knew it, she was nominated to be the vice president of the national organization. When Anne tried to protest, Daisy responded, "Well, you [had] . . . better accept the position . . . or else we will give you a job that really entails some work." Anne reluctantly agreed. She was fond of Daisy, and over the years, she became swept up by the Girl Scout movement, too.

The first troops for younger girls, ages seven to ten, were formed in 1916. They were initially called Junior Girl Scouts, but were later renamed Brownies. Eventually, there would be six categories of Girl Scouts, and the girls would be divided by their grades in school. Even kindergarteners and first-graders could belong to a group, Daisy Girl Scouts.

During the war, Daisy moved the national Girl Scout headquarters to the Harriman National Bank Building at 527 Fifth Avenue in New York City. At one meeting there, the all-female board was evaluating what kind of shoes the girls should wear with their uniforms. Daisy had been testing a pair of the shoes all day. She gathered her skirts around her knees and stood on her head. Then she waggled

Girl Scouts in Savannah practice first aid techniques, using little Johnny Mercer as the patient, circa 1916. Much later, Johnny became a well-known lyricist, songwriter, and singer. *Girl Scouts of the USA–JGLB*

the shoes in the air and claimed they felt quite comfortable. Everyone laughed. Just as Daisy intended, she had reminded the board that Girl Scouting was to be fun. "The girls must always come first," she often said.

Daisy wanted everyone to support her Girl Scouts. One much-repeated story tells of the time Daisy attended a fancy luncheon wearing a hat decorated with vegetables from her kitchen. "Oh, is my trimming sad?" she asked guests as they stared at her. "I can't afford to have this hat done over—I have to save all my money for Girl Scouts." Then Daisy paused dramatically before continuing, "You know about the Scouts, don't you?"

As Eleanor Nash recalled, she was bold, brash, and brave on behalf of the organization. Daisy's behavior amazed her.

I have seen her come into a room full of people who were complete strangers to her, a trying ordeal to many who have sound hearing, and within the space of ten minutes gather the interest of everyone in the room to herself. She did not live alone in her world of silence. She brought the outer world into it with the force of her personality and wit.

At the board's suggestion, the Girl Scouts began their first-ever fundraising campaign in 1917 so that Daisy would not have to continue to bear all the organization's expenses. Anne Hyde Choate and another member formed a committee of two, and they wrote letters asking for contributions of any amount. Donations came in from church members, businesses, and friends, and the Girl Scouts soon had enough money for Daisy to stop worrying about her personal finances.

During this time period, Daisy was also spending as much time as possible with Mamma, who was slowly failing, although she continued to rally after each little spell of illness. Finally, in mid-February 1917, as Nellie Gordon lay in a coma in her upstairs bedroom, her doctor told the family to gather. He thought that she wouldn't last much longer. Everyone rushed to the family home in Savannah. The Gordon children were discussing funeral plans in the downstairs library when suddenly the door opened and Mamma walked in. "I'm not dead yet!" she told her stunned children. "I didn't walk down the stairs," she added. "I slid down the banister!"

Arthur picked up his mother and carried her back upstairs. A few days later, on February 22, she died peacefully in her bed. Eventually, Bill and his wife, Ellie, decided to move into the Gordon home. This pleased Daisy, because it meant that she could visit another generation of children and their parents in the house.

In early 1917, Germany began sinking U.S. ships, and President Wilson finally declared war that April. Following the declaration, the Girl Scouts' National Board of Directors held a meeting. Afterward, the members sent telegrams to the president, offering to help in any way they could. The organization also offered the First Lady, Edith B. Wilson, the position of honorary president of the Girl Scouts. She accepted, and every First Lady to come after her has continued the tradition.

The national headquarters was overwhelmed with requests to start new troops and with ideas for how to help the country during the war. Lou Henry Hoover, who was back in Washington, D.C., with her husband, Herbert, took over as the leader of Troop 8 and instructed her girls to grow vegetables at home in what came to be called victory gardens. As farmers went overseas to fight, food production slowed down, and this caused shortages and even food rationing. Victory gardens helped provide families with low-cost, fresh produce.

Inspired by Mrs. Hoover and her troop, other Girl Scouts began tending backyard gardens, canning fruits and vegetables, and assisting overworked nurses at armed services hospitals as wounded soldiers began returning from Europe in need of extended medical care. The girls also sold war bonds, government-issued savings bonds that helped finance the war. Buying a war bond or tending a victory garden gave all Americans a chance to help at home while the soldiers were fighting in Europe.

Some Girl Scouts worked with the Red Cross, sewing and knitting socks and scarves; others volunteered at canteens inside railroad stations, where they greeted returning soldiers with homemade food and welcoming smiles. Daisy's niece Doots drove vehicles for the Red Cross. Many of the other original Girl Scouts in Savannah, who were then eighteen to twenty-two years old, also volunteered for the Red Cross while the country was at war.

The first known Girl Scout cookie sale took place during this time period, too. The Mistletoe Troop in Muskogee, Oklahoma, baked and sold cookies, and they used some of the money to buy handkerchiefs for U.S. soldiers.

Lou Henry Hoover (left) and her Girl Scout troop tend a victory garden during the Great War. Small plots of fruits and vegetables flourished in vacant lots, backyards, and container pots across the nation. *Herbert Hoover Presidential Library*

Daisy was proud to lead the Girl Scouts into community and national service. She had lived through the Civil War and remembered the positive impact of her volunteer work during the Spanish-American War. Now the Great War was devastating many countries. Daisy wanted more and more young people to befriend one another around the world. She believed that international friendships and understanding others' cultures would encourage peace.

Throughout 1917 and 1918, Daisy was on the road nonstop, delivering speeches about the work of Girl Scouts in nearly every large city in the United States. She had aged, but under her wide-brimmed Scout hat her sparkling dark brown eyes flashed with enthusiasm, and she had an air of authority as powerful as that of any male leader. According to Eleanor Nash, Daisy was "quicksilver and pepper—the whole leavened with humanity and laughter."

Daisy picked the name for a brand-new magazine for the Girl Scouts, *The Rally*, which was first published in 1917 and edited by Helen Ferris. Three years later, the magazine adopted a larger format, with more pictures and a colorful cover, and a committee renamed it *The American Girl*. Daisy graciously admitted that the new name was much better than her original choice. She supervised

In the early days, the Girl Scouts baked sugar cookies in their own kitchens under the supervision of their mothers. Today, the cookies are produced at large bakeries, and the sales fund many Girl Scout activities.
Girl Scouts of the USA–JGLB

revisions of the handbook again, too. Each new edition—and there were several during Daisy's lifetime—reflected the ever-changing roles of young women in American society. One early handbook even mentioned an aviation badge, though flying was still new. Progressive topics such as ecology and organic foods would become part of later editions.

The Great War ended on November 11, 1918. A jubilant Daisy wrote to Mabel from Savannah, saying, "I can see from my front windows crowds and crowds of citizens, on foot, on bicycles, in motors, in street cars with horns, pistols, drums, arching towards the Park! School girls en masse, shipyard laborers, old men and children shouting for joy, women weeping with joy."

In January 1919, the Girl Scout organization released a promotional black-and-white film, *The Golden Eaglet*. Movies were silent at the time, yet wildly popular, and *The Golden Eaglet* was one of the first motion pictures ever produced by a public service organization. It starred real Girl Scouts, and Daisy too, and played before the featured films in theaters across the United States.

Daisy and the other longtime leaders were excited to see how the movie would be received. They believed it would encourage even more young girls to become Girl Scouts in a peaceful postwar environment.

Crowds on Wall Street in New York City celebrated Germany's surrender with flags and confetti. *Library of Congress*

CHAPTER FIFTEEN
Busy on Behalf of Girl Scouts

DURING THE FILM'S RELEASE, Daisy was in England. Agnes Baden-Powell had become vice president of the Girl Guides, and Olave Baden-Powell now headed the organization. Mrs. Baden-Powell suggested that an international body be formed to link the many Girl Scouts and Girl Guides around the world. As a result, the first International Council of Girl Guides and Girl Scouts met in London in February 1919, with Daisy representing the United States of America as president of the Girl Scouts. Nearly fifty countries sent representatives or messages of friendship and peace. Leaders exchanged ideas and experiences and began to plan trips abroad.

While in London after the war, Daisy attended numerous parties and dinners and hosted several of her own. She saw Mabel frequently. And, as she had in the past, Daisy threw theater and dinner parties for Mabel's adult children, Peggy and Rowland, and their friends. Daisy loved to wear her elegant evening clothes for these events.

In a letter to her brother Bill, she wrote, "Everyone [in England] dances . . . a reaction from the awful four years. Staid old generals, old lords, and old ladies like myself included" rolled up the rugs and danced to records on the phonograph. Fifty-eight-year-old Daisy enjoyed some of the popular new dances such as the bunny hop and the turkey trot.

By May, Daisy was back in the United States, along with Robert and Olave Baden-Powell. General Sir Robert Baden-Powell spoke about the Boy Scouts to huge, enthusiastic crowds in Canada and the eastern United States. In Washington, D.C., Mrs. Baden-Powell presented Daisy with the Silver Fish, the highest award given by the Girl Guides in England.

Daisy wearing the Silver Fish. Based on Japanese imagery, the award symbolizes a fish that swims upstream against the current instead of drifting aimlessly downstream. *Corbis*

Days later in New York City's Carnegie Hall, Daisy received a Thanks Badge made of jewels. It was paid for by thousands of Girl Scouts across America who had saved their pennies to show their gratitude to Daisy. She described receiving the honor as "the greatest surprise of my life. . . . I could not speak for joy."

Daisy continued to charge from city to city to promote the Girl Scouts. She always dressed in her Girl Scout uniform, which consisted of a Norfolk-style jacket belted over a white shirt and black tie. A Scout knife, whistle, and drinking cup dangled from her leather belt, and Daisy topped it all with a large hat. As Josephine Daskam Bacon, first chairwoman of the National Publication Committee, noted, Daisy "*loved* her whole uniform."

Many prominent individuals and old friends became increasingly involved in the organization. Lou Henry Hoover accompanied the Girl Scouts on hikes, visited camps, and took part in many ceremonies. She also became a member of the Girl Scout Council in Washington and would later become the third president of the Girl Scouts while her husband served as secretary of commerce under President Warren Harding. However, Anne Hyde Choate saw firsthand that Daisy did everything in the organization's formative years. She observed that Daisy wrote "the Girl Scout literature, acted as its publicity agent, as the one who trained the first captains, as the organizer of the first local councils. . . . She met every demand because she realized the value of the Girl Scout movement for the girls of this country."

Perhaps because of Daisy's total dedication to the movement, it wasn't easy for her to look inward, to see her own quirks. In meetings, she often dominated the discussions, partly because it was so difficult for her to hear the conversations. Some of the ladies complained that it was "hard to straighten her out," while also admitting that Daisy was the "rarest of human beings, an original thinker." Nonetheless, Daisy knew it was time to let others direct and manage the organization. "I realize that each year it has changed and grown until I know that, a decade from now, what I might say of it would seem like an echo of what has been instead of what is."

She resigned as president in 1920, turning over the position to Anne Hyde Choate. Daisy's official title became "founder," which meant that she would continue to represent the Girl Scouting and Girl Guiding movement around the world. Her birthday, October 31, was designated Founder's Day. Girl Scouts are still encouraged to do something special for others on that day, to honor Daisy's lively personality and commitment to the organization.

A dedicated national board and a small band of volunteers continued to run Girl Scouts after Daisy's "retirement." Mrs. Edith Macy of New York was the chairwoman of the board. Jane Deeter Rippin was the national secretary. And Helen Storrow from Massachusetts, or "Aunt Helen," as the Girl Scouts called her, started the first national training camp for troop leaders. On the advice of Lou Henry Hoover, the board also began to hire people to help them run what had been, up until then, primarily a volunteer organization.

Arthur Gordon, Daisy's nephew, recalled, "Girl Scouting, to Daisy, was a grand and glorious game. She was the world's worst organizer, and knew it, but she also knew that vitality and humor and fun are just as important as organization."

When she stepped down as president, there were some 70,000 Girl Scouts nationwide, including the territory of Hawaii. Girls could earn up to twenty-five badges at that time. And a troop for physically challenged Girl Scouts was formed in New York City. An African American troop had started in 1917, and the first Native American troop, consisting of girls from the Onondaga Nation, was formed in central New York State in the 1920s. Mexican American girls in Houston, Texas, also established a troop.

On August 18, 1920, the Nineteenth Amendment gave women the right to vote.

Daisy presents the Founder's Banner to the troop that best upheld the ideals of the Girl Scout organization over the course of the previous year, circa 1922. *Girl Scouts of the USA-JGLB*

Daisy had been working to empower girls around the world for years, and many of those who supported women's right to vote had also supported Daisy's efforts. The Girl Scout organization continued to provide assistance to female voters in the years to come. For example, the October 1924 issue of *Girl Scout Leader* asked Girl Scouts to assist during the presidential election by taking care of small children "so that mothers may go to the polls."

In the early 1920s, the Girl Scouts were beginning to establish "little houses" or "rest houses" across the United States to use for large meetings and training sessions. And Girl Scout camps were cropping up in many places.

Daisy decided she wanted to have a camp on Lookout Mountain in northwest Georgia. After arriving by mule team, she explored the ten acres on foot, with her Pekingese under one arm, and decided to buy it. Camp Juliette Low featured a flat mountaintop and a swimming hole below a rock-strewn hillside.

Miss Daisy became an enthusiastic camper there. Her old friend Dorris Hough recalled her "going with us on our hikes, cooking over our outdoor fires, swimming. . . . She brought her own special bathing suit . . . which had very full, very long bloomers, and a very full, very long skirt adorned with row upon row of white braid."

Miss Hough had been with the Girl Scouts since 1912. She helped Daisy establish Camp Juliette Low and became its director. According to her, Daisy loved to tell fortunes, and "she read the palm of every person in camp, including the boy who brought the milk." Daisy predicted great futures for everyone and shared ghost stories around the evening fires. Daisy also visited other Girl Scout camps around the United States.

In 1922, an American, Anne Mills Archbold, gave the British Girl Guides sixty-five acres of forested land in England that was called Foxlease. There was a cottage on the property for Girl Guides and Girl Scouts to use. The cottage, which Daisy named the Link, is dedicated to her, and is so named to symbolize the bond between Great Britain and the United States. The International Council of Girl Guides and Girl Scouts decided that the first World Camp would be held at Foxlease in 1924.

Daisy was thrilled that the 1922 annual meeting of the Girl Scouts was to be held in Savannah. Because it was in her hometown, she could house some of the visiting delegates, preside over receptions and teas, and generally provide southern hospitality to her guests. By then, the home that she had first shared with Billow had been remodeled, and electric lights had replaced the gas lamps. As usual, Daisy's parrot, Polly Poons, was in her cage on one of the porches, screeching at anyone who passed by. Delegates came from every Girl Scout council, and they stayed at nearby camping areas and in various local homes.

The *Savannah Morning News* reported that on the first day of the meeting Daisy "dashed out . . . in an automobile flying the Girl Scouts' colors, with her guard of honor standing on the running board."

She opened the annual meeting and, relying on her handwritten notes, said, "I did not realize when the first patrol was enrolled here, that the movement would become part of our nation—one unusual thing about Scouting is that its success is due entirely to its members and not to any one man or woman putting it forward." She added, "A few years ago in my ignorance . . . I said, 'as soon as I get 100,000 members, I will die.' . . . We now number more than 113,000 & I am not prepared to die yet."

To raise money for activities, more Girl Scouts and their mothers began to bake simple shortbread cookies at home. In the 1920s and the early 1930s, trefoil-shaped cookies were sealed in bags made of brown or wax paper and sold door-to-door for twenty-five to thirty cents per dozen. Starting in 1936, a nationwide program began, with a professional baker making the cookies, and the girls still sell them today.

For a number of years, on October 31, Daisy wrote a birthday message to the Girl Scouts. Her 1923 message, which appeared in *The American Girl*, read, in part,

My Dear Girl Scouts,
Little did I dream, when I myself was young and tried these Halloween pranks, that I should live to see that day turned into a Girl Scout Founder's Day. So you will understand what a thrill of gratitude comes over me.
One's birthday should be the day for good resolutions.

Daisy suggested that each girl put herself in another's place to understand human relationships.

To put yourself in another's place requires real imagination, but by so doing each Girl Scout will be able to live among others happily.
Your friend,
Juliette Low.

By 1923, or possibly even earlier, Daisy learned that she had breast cancer. Since she didn't write about it or share the news with her siblings, we know few details about her condition. In those days, people usually didn't talk or write about chronic illnesses.

According to her niece Peggy Leigh Graves, Daisy had an operation in January 1924. At that time, she wrote a letter to each of her brothers and sisters in case anything should happen to her.

I look forward to seeing the parents, Willy Low, Alice . . . and all the people I have loved and lost. I've always dreaded growing old and being a burden to my family. You and yours have always been so good to me that I can't thank you enough.

Luckily, she survived the operation and the letters did not have to be sent.

By June she was as active as ever, giving speeches on behalf of the Scouting movement. At Mercer University in Macon, Georgia, Daisy said that the Girl Scout badges "mean nothing in themselves . . . but they mark a certain achievement." Daisy envisioned a much bigger picture for her girls and told her audience, "Scouting is the cradle of careers. It is where careers are born." She spoke of young Girl Scouts earning a Red Cross badge by learning how to bandage an injured person, which could lead them to careers in nursing. Or after learning the Morse code, girls might consider future jobs as telegraph operators.

Legendary New York Yankees baseball player Babe Ruth publicizes the Girl Scouts' cookie sale by eating a cookie at the last game of the 1923 World Series. *Girl Scouts of the USA-JGLB. Used by permission from Major League Baseball Properties.*

Daisy talks to the American delegation at the first World Camp, at Foxlease, England, in July 1924. *Girl Scouts of the USA-JGLB*

That fall, Daisy approached Peggy, who at the time didn't know about her aunt's previous surgery, for advice. Peggy was a nurse, and she worked at a children's hospital in London. "Aunt Daisy confided to me—under a bond of secrecy—that she was worried about her health."

Daisy wanted to know about British doctors and hospitals, but only if Peggy promised not to tell Mabel or anyone else in the Gordon family about her illness. Peggy recommended a doctor, who led Daisy to a famous surgeon, coincidentally named Dr. Low. He convinced Daisy that she needed another operation immediately.

Daisy, with her unique style of spelling, wrote to Peggy on October 21, 1924, the day before she underwent surgery for the second time.

Darling Peggie,

Don't imagine that I am <u>coragous</u>, because I am really glad to go to that "Promised Land", and like Bro' Rabbit and the Briar Patch all I want is to be flung in the Briar Patch—for we must all die and when one is ready, its so more satisfactory to peg out while one is still beloved.

I hope and pray, if I come through tomorrow, that I should live, to a green old age, I will still have the love which you have given me today— Thank you from the depths of my heart,

Always your loving Aunt Daisy

CHAPTER SIXTEEN

Camp Macy

AFTER THE SURGERY, Daisy returned to her London home on Grosvenor Square. No one saw her at first, not even Peggy. Only Bella, Daisy's trusted maid, cared for her immediately following the operation.

About ten days later, Peggy received a call from Aunt Daisy while she was at work. "Hullo Peggy, I'm home. . . . I want you to come right on over. . . . I will expect you in about twenty minutes. Take a taxi." She hung up before Peggy could even speak.

So Peggy came, as did Daisy's doctor, Bruce Williamson. Daisy insisted they open a bottle of champagne. "Champagne is for parties and this is one," she said. Much later, Peggy would realize that her aunt insisted on the champagne party so her niece would think that the operation had cured her health issues.

However, it had not. Peggy and Daisy later went to Liverpool together, without telling anyone why. Daisy wanted to try a new treatment Dr. Williamson had recommended. She stayed at a nursing home in Liverpool for ten days; Peggy stayed at a hotel but "spent each day with her, going with her when she had her treatment."

Family members began to notice that Daisy did not look well, but everyone in the family knew better than to ask about it. In a letter to her brother Arthur, Daisy downplayed the situation, saying only that she had had a pea-size lump removed from her neck. But in reality, the surgery and treatments were not successful.

Despite her poor health, Daisy plunged back into her hectic lifestyle, enjoying frequent luncheons and parties. To Mabel, she wrote, "Every place I visit brings more luck to me in scouting." Mrs. Hoover took Daisy and several others to the White House, where they visited with the First Lady and "enrolled Mrs. Coolidge as a Girl Scout! She has promised to be honorary president," Daisy wrote.

She fished with her nephew Arthur, wearing a floppy hat to protect her skin from the Savannah sun and layers of mosquito netting to keep the bugs away. And she continued to throw parties. Once, according to her nephew Rowland, Daisy invited him to one at her home. All the guests had arrived, but there was no sign

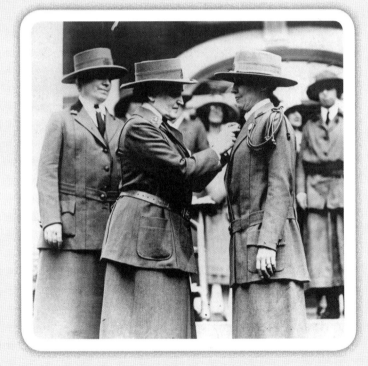

With Lou Henry Hoover looking on, Daisy pins the Tenderfoot Badge on First Lady Grace Coolidge, honorary president of the Girl Scouts. *Girl Scouts of the USA–JGLB*

of his aunt. He found her upstairs in her bed, going over her bills. Because of her hearing impairment, Daisy had not heard anyone arrive. Rowland reminded her that she was giving a dance party.

"Why, so I am!" she said. "I'll be down in five minutes."

Daisy also continued to journey back and forth between Europe and the United States. In England, she attended a meeting of the International Council of Girl Guides, where it was proposed that the fourth World Camp be held in Switzerland. Daisy didn't like the idea at all. She convinced the council that it was America's turn and promised that the Girl Scouts would pay the travel expenses for one delegate from every country. And then, in the spring of 1925, she sailed home to the United States.

"I have a wonderful new plan!" Daisy told Jane Deeter Rippin, who was then the national director of Girl Scouts. "Just think, Jane, we are going to have the World Camp here in America next year! Everything is arranged."

At the time, the Girl Scouts owned four hundred acres of undeveloped country property in New York State. The land was a recent gift from V. Everitt Macy to the Girl Scouts in honor of his late wife, Edith, who had been the chairwoman of the executive committee for many years. Girl Scout leaders intended to develop what would be called Camp Edith Macy by 1928. But Daisy thought it would only take a year to construct some simple buildings and a road and drill for water, so that Camp Macy could open in May 1926. Daisy convinced Jane Deeter Rippin and the rest of the executive board of the Girl Scouts to go forward and host the International Conference of Girl Guides and Girl Scouts there. Then she told the executive board to expect between three hundred and four hundred girls. She'd already started to invite them!

On February 12, 1926, while the camp was being readied, the city of Savannah honored Daisy for her service. A large crowd made up of Boy Scouts, Girl Scouts, city leaders, and friends gathered in Forsyth Park. Daisy received flowers, many congratulatory telegrams, and a proclamation from the city in appreciation of all her work with the Girl Scouts.

Accompanied by Olave Baden-Powell, fifty-six delegates from twenty-nine countries arrived in New York on the SS *Olympic* on May 5. Waiting American Girl Scouts stood on the pier and waved handkerchiefs at them. Mary Lagercrantz, chief guide of Sweden, wrote that they drove up Fifth Avenue "without stopping once, the traffic being held up for [them], people staring. Was it not a thoroughly American welcome, thrilling and unusual?" The Manhattan Girl Scout Council held a luncheon in their honor, and a beaming Daisy gave a welcoming speech to her foreign guests. Over the next few days, they toured New York, Boston, and Washington, D.C., where President and Mrs. Coolidge also received them for lunch. On May 11, a motorcade carrying Girl Guides from dozens of countries headed to Camp Macy.

It was a glorious day in New York State. Daisy didn't want to miss a single detail of this opening day. Her driver steered up the steep dirt road leading to the entrance gate of Camp Edith Macy. Daisy leaned way out the window of her car to look behind her as the line of vehicles followed her up the hill.

Recent rains had soaked the campground and the surrounding landscape, turning the soil velvet brown. Woods, mixed with rolling hills and deep ravines, stretched out in every direction. But now, under a blue canopy of sky lit by the afternoon sun, dogwood and apple trees bloomed. Fuzzy-looking new grass poked up through the wet ground.

Ahead, Daisy saw the Great Hall, where they would all gather that night. She

160

spotted cabins, and tents sporting clean white canvas tops. She pictured the rows of waiting cots and the carefully folded blankets inside each one.

Just a few days earlier, well diggers on the property had finally struck water. Daisy didn't understand why her dear friends on the executive board had fussed so much about finding water and other details. Everything had turned out perfectly, just as she had known it would. She hadn't worried a bit!

At the top of a rise, Daisy's car stopped. She stepped out quickly, ready to greet the visitors in the motorcade. Miss Daisy waved to a group of experienced American Girl Scouts lining the edge of the road. They too were waiting for the newcomers to arrive, eager to help them settle in.

Standing in front of the Great Hall at Camp Macy in 1926, Girl Scouts and Girl Guides hold flags representing their countries. *Girl Scouts of the USA-NHPC*

Though she could not hear them, Daisy imagined the sounds of the flags snapping in the breeze, just as she imagined bees buzzing in the flowering trees. Her dear friends Robert and Olave Baden-Powell stood at her side with the members of the executive board. Together they welcomed each girl, starting with the fifty-six foreign delegates.

Later, Olave recalled how B-P, Daisy, and Anne Hyde Choate "strolled along the sandy lane, the bushes swaying in the wind, and the country all ablaze with the glory of the spring. How *happy* [Daisy] was! Her wish had been fulfilled."

That night, the official opening of Camp Macy was celebrated in the Great Hall. Construction had been completed just in the nick of time. Jane Deeter Rippin noted, "We bowed the plasterers out the back door while we welcomed our guests in at the front."

Olave and Robert Baden-Powell, arm in arm, with Anne Hyde Choate to the left. *Girl Scouts of the USA-NHPC*

The girls in attendance were especially eager to hear Miss Daisy's campfire stories. Fires crackled in five enormous stone fireplaces. Daisy began, her voice animated, as though she were talking for the very first time about her great-grandmother, Little Ship Under Full Sail, or about her haunted castle in Scotland. The girls leaned forward, listening eagerly, even though some had heard Miss Daisy share the same stories around other campfires. Daisy was surrounded by her ever-expanding family of Girl Scouts, and she loved them as if they were her own children.

Everyone who later wrote about the World Camp remembered that Daisy radiated joy that entire week. She chatted with the campers and worked and planned future activities for "her girls." Those who watched her or received her warm embrace that first day or on the days that followed were caught up in her infectious excitement and enthusiasm. They expected her to be involved with Girl Scouts for years to come.

But Daisy knew it wasn't to be. At night, she collapsed onto her bed in a little white farmhouse that belonged to the camp. Only a few close friends knew that every minute of every day, Daisy was in pain.

As the week at Camp Macy drew to a close, the young attendees began to dread the inevitable separation from their new friends. How would a girl from Germany stay connected to her friend from Canada or from Denmark, or from South Africa or China, so far away?

A French girl suggested a solution. During one of the final sessions, she proposed that one day of the year should be set aside for all Girl Guides and Girls Scouts to think of one another. That would make their parting much easier. Everyone, especially Daisy, loved the idea. February 22 became Thinking Day and was later renamed World Thinking Day.

After the World Camp, Daisy headed to Savannah. Then, according to her brother Arthur, she traveled to Richmond, Virginia. Her brother-in-law, Dr. Stuart McGuire, was in charge of a medical clinic there, and she underwent some kind of treatment or perhaps a consultation.

While at the clinic, she was expected to stay in bed and rest. Not Daisy! She had too much to do. One day, she dressed in her uniform and slipped out and into a waiting taxi to attend a Girl Scout conference. Informed of her escape, Dr. McGuire said, "Let her alone. If she wanted to go that badly, it will do her no harm."

Daisy gave a lively, informative talk to the girls at the conference before returning to the clinic and falling into bed. As she often said, "We mustn't lose sight of the girls."

Daisy knew she had inoperable cancer, yet she was still hoping for a cure and continued her treatments. There were several things she wanted to accomplish in her remaining time. In England, she settled her business affairs. She finished sculpting and casting a bronze bust of her Grandfather Gordon, had it packed, and shipped it back to the United States.

She also attended a musical performance of *Charlot Revue,* for which her nephew Rowland Leigh had written some of the songs. Daisy had front-row seats, and she arrived with ten deaf people. They all brought the latest in hearing machines and ear trumpets so they could enjoy the music, dances, and skits.

By then, Daisy was sixty-six years old and her condition had worsened. She returned to the States and was eager to get back home to Savannah. But first, she visited her sister Nell in New Jersey and called Anne Hyde Choate and some other Girl Scout leaders. Once again, she announced, "I have a wonderful plan for Girl

Scouts!" Daisy wanted to be sure that an idea of Mrs. Hoover's, to hold regional conferences in Mexico, Canada, and other neighboring countries in the Western Hemisphere, would actually come to fruition.

That Christmas, Daisy wrote checks to her family and sent them with cheerful letters. Her brother Arthur somehow discovered the truth about her health and called everyone home to Savannah, saying, "Daisy has only six weeks to live." Mabel and her daughter Peggy sailed for America.

And the sad news spread. Notes of love from Girl Scouts, friends, and family overflowed Daisy's mailbox. She laughed about all the flowers that arrived. "There won't be any left for the funeral if this keeps up!" Her nephew Arthur would later write, "[Aunt Daisy] was always . . . roaring with laughter, often self-directed."

On January 16, Daisy changed her will, making sure everyone in the family received something. She left the house to her brother Bill's deaf son, also named Bill, knowing he might need extra financial help. The last paragraph of her will read, "I trust I have left no enmities; and I leave and bequeath to my family my friendships, especially my beloved Girl Scouts."

To Mary Gale Carter, her dear school friend and the mother of Anne Hyde Choate, she wrote, "How nice it is to believe we may meet in the future for we have loved each other many years, and our love will endure after death. . . . Give my love to Anne, and make her realize that when she took up Girl Scouts, she gave me one of the happiest hours in my life. I can't write more just now."

Family members filled the house, weeping, hugging, mending any rifts, and saying their final goodbyes. Then, on January 17, 1927, Daisy died as she wished, at home in Savannah.

After everyone else left, Peggy Graves lingered for a moment in her aunt's bedroom. Daisy's well-worn Bible, bound in crocodile skin, sat on the bedside table. Peggy "stood at attention and saluted [Aunt Daisy and] . . . suddenly realized that she was smiling as if she had found something very lovely at the end of her journey."

Juliette Gordon Low's funeral service was at Christ Church in Savannah. Some two hundred Girl Scouts lined up along each side of the steps leading to the church's doors. They ranged from the youngest girls, the Brownies, on up in rank to the Golden Eaglets. Family, friends, Girl Scouts, and community leaders filled the pews.

Local Girl Scouts formed an honor guard at Christ Church in Savannah for Daisy's memorial service.
Girl Scouts of the USA–JGLB

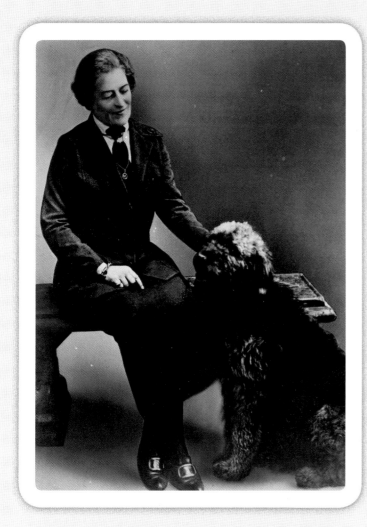

This was Daisy's favorite photograph of herself. *Girl Scouts of the USA-JGLB*

Roses and lilies covered her coffin. Above, in the choir loft, the Girl Scout flag was draped beside the American flag. The solemn but simple candlelit afternoon ceremony ended with one of Daisy's favorite hymns, "Fight the Good Fight."

Daisy was laid to rest under the great magnolia trees in Laurel Grove Cemetery, near her parents and her sister Alice. As she had requested, she was buried in her Girl Scout uniform, wearing the insignia of her beloved organization, including the Silver Fish and the jeweled Thanks Badge.

Again at her request, a telegram was tucked into her uniform pocket. It had come from her dear friend Anne Hyde Choate, but it expressed the words of everyone on the Girl Scout National Council. It read:

You are not only the first Girl Scout but the best Girl Scout of them all.

CHAPTER SEVENTEEN

A Big Little Woman's Legacy

WHEN DAISY DIED IN 1927, there were about 168,000 Girl Scouts in the United States. She left these young women in good hands, to be led by many of her friends and relatives at the national level, and by dedicated adult leaders in small towns and cities around the country. Daisy would be delighted to know that there are now approximately 3.4 million girls and adults actively involved in Girl Scouts. Her dream for "all of America" and the entire world has come true.

Girl Scouting first came to America in 1912, inspired by the British Girl Guides. But it wasn't until 1932 that March 12, 1912, was designated the official birthday of the Girl Scouts. In 1947, the name was formally changed to the Girl Scouts of the USA (GSUSA).

The GSUSA is a nonprofit organization and the largest voluntary organization for girls in the world. It belongs to the World Association of Girl Guides and Girl Scouts

(WAGGGS), a worldwide family of 10 million girls and adults in 145 countries. WAGGGS is the successor to the International Council of Girl Guides and Girl Scouts that Juliette Gordon Low, Olave Baden-Powell, and others created in 1920.

The GSUSA National Headquarters and the National Historic Preservation Center (NHPC), the department of GSUSA where the archives are kept, are in New York City. There are more than one hundred councils throughout the United States, supporting more than 200,000 local troops. Girl Scouts also live in United States territories and overseas in some ninety countries. Every American First Lady, starting with Edith Wilson in 1917, has served as the honorary president of the Girl Scouts.

This 1935 billboard invites young women to join Girl Scouts and "build character." *Georgia Historical Society*

The quickest way to learn all about Girl Scouts is to visit their website, www.girlscouts.org. Another way is to find a local Girl Scout council and contact the leader of a troop. In spite of the many changes between Daisy's era and now, the Girl Scouts still strongly support her firm belief that it's all about the girls. She wanted her girls to have fun and form friendships while building character and self-worth and helping out in their community. They still do all these things today.

Girl Scouts is open to girls of all races and religious beliefs from kindergarten through high school, ages five to seventeen, including young women with physical or developmental disabilities. The GSUSA values diversity and inclusiveness and has adopted a strong official inclusion statement. A girl can join a troop or work independently as a "Juliette." Women and men over the age of seventeen can join the organization as adult volunteers. Troops are organized by grade:

- Girl Scout Daisy — Grades K–1
- Girl Scout Brownie — Grades 2–3
- Girl Scout Junior — Grades 4–5
- Girl Scout Cadette — Grades 6–8
- Girl Scout Senior — Grades 9–10
- Girl Scout Ambassador — Grades 11–12

The National Board of Directors runs the GSUSA, and they often reach out to the young Girl Scouts, volunteers, and staff throughout the organization to get feedback. This partnership between the national office and the local troops has resulted in a more modern leadership philosophy based on a renewed commitment to the values inherent in the Girl Scout Promise and Law. The current Promise and Law read:

The Girl Scout Promise

On my honor, I will try:
To serve God* and my country,
To help people at all times,
And to live by the Girl Scout Law.

The Girl Scout Law

I will do my best to be
honest and fair,
friendly and helpful,
considerate and caring,
courageous and strong, and
responsible for what I say and do,
and to
respect myself and others,
respect authority,
use resources wisely,
make the world a better place, and
be a sister to every Girl Scout.

---

* According to the GSUSA, the word *God* can be interpreted in a number of ways, depending on one's spiritual beliefs. When reciting the Girl Scout Promise, it is okay to replace the word *God* with whatever word your spiritual beliefs dictate.

In 2006, the organization adopted the mission statement "Girl Scouting builds girls of courage, confidence, and character, who make the world a better place." This is exactly what Daisy envisioned when she first became involved with Girl Guides in Great Britain.

Girl Scouting continues to emphasize a healthy lifestyle and outdoor activities, such as camping, canoeing, and bird watching. Girls still earn badges in these areas, as well as in first aid, cooking, and infant care. During Daisy's time, there were only a few dozen badges; now there are hundreds. Many of the current ones are designed to be appropriate for the needs of a particular age group, and they often reflect the changing times. Girls might earn a badge by participating in environmental events like planting a tree or studying native plants, or work on a music-related badge by making an instrument or attending a ballet or opera. They can learn to surf, design jewelry, or help out at a local animal shelter. Older girls might work on breast cancer awareness or aviation, or learn about teen pregnancy and AIDS.

Daisy's original vision included getting girls involved in many outdoor activities. This was unusual in 1913, when this photograph was probably taken. *Girl Scouts of the USA-JGLB*

Girl Scouts can communicate with other Girl Scouts online, and they can even earn badges by using the Internet, often guided by an adult leader. For example, the Sky Search badge directs the girls to planetarium websites so they can gain a better understanding of stargazing, constellations, and star maps.

The Gold Award is now the highest honor earned in Girl Scouting. It is given to a Girl Scout who creates change by developing and implementing a project that fulfills a particular need in her community. The young women who earn the Gold Award are typically juniors or seniors in high school, and they choose to finish their Girl Scouting experience by doing something meaningful, such as working with incarcerated mothers, helping children in low-income schools improve their literacy, or gathering and organizing library books for hospice patients.

Thinking Day was first commemorated on February 22, 1927, a few weeks after Daisy's death. And Girl Scouts still celebrate Founder's Day every October 31. Both days are part of the extensive calendar of Girl Scout council events, including the annual Girl Scout Week celebration in March. In addition to being active in a local troop or council, the girls have the opportunity to attend Girl Scout camps around the country, conferences, and events at four international WAGGGS Centers: Our Chalet, in Adelboden, Switzerland; Pax Lodge, outside of London, England; Our Cabaña, near Cuernavaca, Mexico; and Sangam, close to Poona, India.

Savannah, Georgia, is a popular destination for thousands of Girl Scouts. The Juliette Gordon Low Birthplace, her family home, is located in the heart of the city's historic district, and is now a National Historic Landmark and a Girl Scout National Program Center. Built in 1821, the Wayne-Gordon House is at 10 East Oglethorpe Avenue. At the museum there, tours are conducted and educational programs given for Girl Scouts, their families, and individuals. Interpretive staff lead tours through the house, which is furnished as it appeared in 1886. Visitors love their funny and lively stories about Juliette Low and the Gordon family. Some of Daisy's art is exhibited inside the house, including two sets of hand-painted dinner plates. And the iron gates that she forged for Wellesbourne House in England are displayed in the garden. The museum store is a popular part of the site.

President Harry Truman signed the bill authorizing the release of this stamp to honor what would have been Juliette Gordon Low's eighty-eighth birthday on October 31, 1948. *From the collection of Hal G. Evarts Jr.*

The Andrew Low House is also located in Savannah at 329 Abercorn Street. Guided tours feature antique furnishings and the Low family history. Guests enjoy hearing about some of the home's famous visitors, such as Robert E. Lee, and learn about Daisy's life as a newlywed in this house.

Behind the Low House, at 330 Drayton Street, is a carriage house, built in 1848. In 1912, Daisy converted the building into what is now called the Girl Scout First Headquarters (FHQ). It was willed to the Girl Scouts of Savannah upon her death and is run by the Girl Scouts of Historic Georgia. It opened on January 15, 1996, as a Girl Scout museum, and it houses archives documenting the Savannah Girl Scouts from 1912 to the present. Visitors can take a self-guided tour, and troops can participate in interactive programs there.

This photograph shows Daisy (fourth from left, back row) with a Girl Scout troop at the headquarters building behind her house in Savannah. *Girl Scouts of the USA–JGLB*

Besides these three sites associated with Juliette Low, visitors can go to Laurel Grove Cemetery, where the Gordon family graves are located, and to Christ Church, where Daisy was christened, married, and memorialized after her death. Daisy's hometown is a primary destination for heritage and cultural tourism, with lots of places to explore.

Although box designs and cookie recipes have changed, Girl Scout cookie sales continue. About two hundred million boxes of cookies are sold each year. *The Rally*, which became *The American Girl* magazine, is no longer published. But today there are many new program-related materials, handbooks, and web pages for the

A group of Girl Scouts read *The American Girl*, one of the nation's first magazines for girls, at Camp Juliette Low in 1923. *Girl Scouts of the USA-NHPC*

Girl Scouts and their adult leaders. Girl Scouts can also participate in leadership journeys, coordinated series of activities grouped around a theme.

As friends and family recalled, Daisy loved her uniform and everything that went with it, including her knife and tin cup. She would have been fascinated with the new badges, patches, and pins, as well as with the many styles and colors of uniforms that girls have worn since 1927. Juliette Gordon Low has received numerous posthumous honors, which she also would have enjoyed.

But perhaps Josephine Daskam Bacon, an early member of the Girl Scout National Board of Directors and the first chair of the Publicity Committee, honored Daisy best when she called her friend "a big little woman" who stepped into many roles as a "dauntless little Joan of Arc, planting her precious [Girl Scout] banner all over the country; a broadminded administrator, adapting herself shrewdly to changing conditions; [and] a gracious Southern woman, honoring her friends with every means in her hands. . . . It will be hard for those she brought together to forget her," Mrs. Bacon concluded.

Daisy never forgot her three Girl Guide patrols in Great Britain or her first two patrols in Savannah, Georgia. In fact, she kept in close contact with the girls by visiting them and writing them letters. As the organization grew, she tried to meet as many other Girl Scouts as she could at conferences and camps, around campfires, and wherever girls gathered. It would be a huge job for Daisy to stay connected today, since the Girl Scouts of the USA has over fifty million alumni, including the former secretary of state Madeleine Albright; America's first female Supreme Court justice, Sandra Day O'Connor; the television personality Katie Couric; the Olympic gold

In this photo taken circa 1913, Daisy is surrounded by dozens of Girl Scouts, doing what she loved best: being with "her girls." *Girl Scouts of the USA–JGLB*

medalist Jackie Joyner-Kersee; the NASA astronaut Sally Ride; the actress and singer Keke Palmer; and the actresses Dakota and Elle Fanning and Reese Witherspoon. But knowing Daisy, she would find a way to befriend *all* the alumni and the more than three million active Girl Scouts and their leaders. *I have a plan,* she might tell a friend.

AUTHOR'S NOTE

TUESDAYS WERE OUR MEETING DAYS, right after school in our local La Jolla Community Center. I belonged to Troop 695. La Jolla is a sleepy beach town in Southern California, where the weather is nice nearly 365 days a year. We swam in the Pacific Ocean, hiked throughout San Diego County, camped in the nearby desert, and collected mistletoe in the backcountry that we sold in ribbon-bedecked bunches. We enjoyed dinner dances with our fathers, put on fashion shows with our mothers, marched in our uniforms in the local parade, and sang endless Girl Scout songs.

For two summers in a row, I attended a weeklong Brownie camp in the nearby Cuyamaca Mountains, where I passed a swimming test, made a tulle doll, and had a wonderful time.

As Girl Scouts, we worked on earning new badges, and the last one was for cycling. Sleek-looking ten-speed bicycles were just becoming popular at the time, and eventually we each earned enough money to buy one. We practiced endlessly and pedaled everywhere in our county until we achieved our goal: to bicycle fifty miles in four hours.

We joined the American Youth Hostel (AYH), an organization we had studied to get our cycling badge. During the summer of 1960, Ann Boughton, our longtime leader, rented an AYH bus that had S-shaped hooks in the back where we could hang our thirty-some bicycles. We stowed our gear and food below them, and off we went! For five glorious weeks, we rode in the bus on highways and cycled on country roads

This is a picture of the Girl Scouts in front of the AYH bus in 1960. I'm fourth from the right. *Author's collection*

Many of the members of Troop 695 gathered at a recent Girl Scout reunion. I'm at the top left. *Author's collection*

from Southern California to western Canada and back while camping in state and national parks each night. In that pre–cell phone era, our parents received only the occasional postcard. The experience was life-changing.

We sang many songs on the bus and around campfires, but there is one, about making new friends and keeping the old, that I will never forget. Our friendships were formed as Brownies and Girl Scouts in the 1950s and 1960s, and now, many decades later, we remain treasured friends. We visit one another, send e-mails, and exchange news about our significant others, our families, and now our grandchildren.

And yes, we hold reunions. We bring our photo albums, show off our badge-decorated sashes, still sing those familiar songs, and know that our friendships began with Troop 695.

Thank you, Juliette Gordon Low!

MAKE NEW FRIENDS

Traditional

D   A⁷   D

1. Make new friends and keep the old. One is sil- ver and the oth- er gold.

2. A circle's round; it has no end.
   That's how long I want to be your friend.

3. A fire burns bright; it warms the heart.
   We've been friends from the very start.

4. You have one hand, I have the other.
   Put them together and we have each other.

5. Silver is precious; gold is, too.
   I am precious and so are you.

CHRONOLOGY

1857	December 21: William (Willie) Washington Gordon and Eleanor (Nellie) Lytle Kinzie marry.
1858	September 27: Eleanor Gordon is born, nicknamed Nell.
1860	October 31: Juliette Magill Kinzie Gordon is born, nicknamed Daisy.
	November 6: Abraham Lincoln elected president of the United States.
1861	April 12: Fort Sumter fired upon, essentially starting the Civil War.
1863	August 7: Sarah Alice Gordon is born, called Alice.
1864	December 21: Union troops march into Savannah and the city surrenders.
1865	January: Daisy, her mother, and siblings go to stay with Grandmother Juliette Augusta Magill Kinzie (Ganny) and Grandfather John Harris Kinzie in Chicago.
	April 9: The Civil War ends.
	April 14: President Abraham Lincoln is shot; he dies April 15.
	June 21: Grandfather Kinzie dies.
1866	April 16: William Washington Gordon III is born, called Bill.
1870	September 15: Ganny Kinzie dies.
	October 28: Mabel McLane Gordon is born.
1872	August 30: George Arthur Gordon, the youngest child of Willie and Nellie Gordon, is born, called Arthur.
circa 1873	Daisy starts boarding school at the Virginia Female Institute, now Stuart Hall School in Staunton, Virginia.
1879	Daisy begins attending Mesdemoiselles Charbonniers' finishing school in New York City.
1880	December 30: Sarah Alice Gordon dies of scarlet fever.
1885	January: Daisy becomes partially deaf in one ear.

1886	December 21: Daisy marries William Mackay Low.
	Late December: Daisy becomes totally deaf in other ear.
1896	April 6 to 15: First International Olympic games held in the modern era, in Athens, Greece.
1898	April 21: Spanish-American War starts.
	Summer: Daisy returns to the United States and, with her mother, cares for soldiers in a hospital in Florida.
1905	June 8: William Mackay Low dies.
1907	August: Robert Baden-Powell's experimental camp for boys is established at Brownsea Island in southern England. This is considered the unofficial start of Boy Scouts.
1908	September: Organized Boy Scouts commence with the opening of an office in London.
	Scouting for Boys is published by Robert Baden-Powell.
1910	Girl Guide movement and organization starts in England.
1911	May 11: Daisy meets General Sir Robert Baden-Powell, founder of Boy Scouts in Great Britain and other countries, and his sister Agnes, first president of Girl Guides in Great Britain.
	August: Daisy organizes a Girl Guide patrol in Glen Lyon, Scotland.
	Fall: Daisy organizes two patrols in London.
1912	March 12: Daisy's niece, Margaret "Daisy Doots" Gordon, becomes the first registered Girl Guide in America. Seventeen other girls also register on that day.
	April 15: The *Titanic* sinks in the Atlantic on its maiden voyage.
	September 11: William Washington Gordon II dies.
1913	June: National Headquarters established in Washington, D.C.
	The handbook *How Girls Can Help Their Country* is published.
	Girl Scouts becomes the new name for Girl Guides in America.

1914   February: Trefoil design for membership badge is patented.

Summer: Great War in Europe begins (later called World War I).

1915   June 15: Girl Scout organization is incorporated.

June: Daisy elected president of Girl Scouts. Girl Scout bylaws and constitution
     adopted at first annual convention in Washington, D.C.

Daisy sells her string of pearls to fund the Girl Scouts' operating expenses
     for another year.

1916   April: Girl Scout headquarters moved to New York City.

Total of seven thousand girls enrolled in Girl Scouts.

First African American troops begin to form.

1917   February 22: Nellie Kinzie Gordon dies.

April 6: The United States enters World War I.

Spring: Edith Wilson, as First Lady, becomes the first honorary national president
     of Girl Scouts.

October: Monthly publication of *The Rally* begins.

First troop of physically handicapped girls is organized in New York City.

1918   Fall: *The Golden Eaglet,* the first film about the Girl Scouts, is shot on location
     in New York State.

November 11: World War I ends.

In recognition of Girl Scout bond sales totaling over $9 million during the war,
     the United States Treasury strikes the Girl Scout Liberty Loan Medal.

1919   February: First meeting of the International Council of Girl Guides and Girl
     Scouts is held in London, England.

October: First nationwide celebration of Girl Scout Week.

1920	January: Daisy retires as president, takes title of Founder of Girl Scouts.
	July: First International Conference of Girl Guides and Girl Scouts is held in Oxford, England, and a delegation of American Girl Scouts attends.
	August 18: Nineteenth Amendment passes, giving women the right to vote.
	October 31: Founder's Day is established in Girl Scouts.
	The Rally becomes *The American Girl* magazine.
	Scouting for Girls: Official Handbook of the Girl Scouts, edited by Josephine Daskam Bacon, is published.
	Badges in this decade show the changing times. Examples: Economist and Motorist badges.
1921	Camp Andree Clark, the first national Girl Scout camp, opens at Briarcliff Manor, New York.
1922	April: Publication of the monthly Girl Scout bulletin, *Field News*, begins.
	Camp Juliette Low in Cloudland, Georgia, is personally established by Daisy.
1923	December: *Field News* is renamed *Girl Scout Leader* (later renamed *Leader*).
1926	May: Fourth International Conference of Girl Guides and Girl Scouts and second World Camp, both the first in the United States, held at Camp Edith Macy in Briarcliff Manor, New York. Representatives from twenty-nine countries attend.
1927	January 17: Juliette Gordon Low dies.
	February 22: First Thinking Day is celebrated.
	Juliette Gordon Low World Friendship Fund started in Daisy's honor.
	American girls living abroad first register as Troops on Foreign Soil (TOFS).
1928	May: World Association of Girl Guides and Girl Scouts (WAGGGS) is formed.
1929	First Lady Lou Henry Hoover, already active in Girl Scouting, gives the organization even more prestige.

1929 (cont.)   First entirely Native American Girl Scout troop registers in central New York State.

By the end of the year, there are 200,000 Girl Scouts.

1932   March 12 is designated as the official birthday of Girl Scouts.

1936   First national sale of Girl Scout cookies.

1940   The Brownie Girl Scout category for ages seven to ten is added.

1942   October: *Volunteers for Victory*, a motion picture showcasing the important work of Girl Scouts in support of the World War II effort, and a plea for leaders, is released.

1944   March 12: President Franklin Roosevelt honors the Girl Scouts for donating over 15 million hours of service during the war effort since 1941.

May 12: The SS *Juliette Low*, a Liberty ship for the Merchant Marines, is launched.

1947   November 24: Name officially changes to Girl Scouts of the USA (GSUSA).

1948   October 29: The U.S. Post Office Department issues a three-cent commemorative stamp honoring Juliette Gordon Low.

1950   By the end of the year, there are 1.5 million Girl Scouts and adult volunteers.

1953   January: National Historic Preservation Center is established at the GSUSA National Headquarters in New York City.

December: Daisy's birthplace in Savannah, Georgia, is purchased by the GSUSA.

1956   October 19: Juliette Gordon Low Birthplace is dedicated as a Girl Scout National Program Center and a historic house museum for the public.

1960s   Four program age levels are established: Brownie, Junior, Cadette, and Senior Girl Scouts.

National Board strongly supports efforts to pass the Civil Rights Act.

1973   March 28: Portrait of Juliette Gordon Low by Edward Hughes is presented to the National Portrait Gallery in Washington, D.C.

1974   Bust of Juliette Gordon Low is placed in the Georgia Hall of Fame at the Georgia
        state capitol.

1975   November: Gloria D. Scott, the first African American national president of GSUSA,
        is elected.

1979   October 28: Daisy is inducted into the National Women's Hall of Fame in Seneca
        Falls, New York.

1983   December: The Juliette Gordon Low Federal Complex opens in Savannah, Georgia,
        the second federal building to be named after a woman.

1992   July: National Headquarters of GSUSA moves to its current location at 420 Fifth
        Avenue in New York City.

1999   November: Connie Matsui, the first Asian American National President of GSUSA,
        is elected.

2005   October 14: Daisy is honored with a large bronze medallion set on the Extra Mile
        Points of Light Volunteer Pathway near the White House in Washington, D.C.

2009   October 29: President Barack Obama signs the Girl Scouts of the USA Commemorative
        Coin Act to authorize the minting of 350,000 silver dollar coins. The coin honors
        Girl Scouts and the achievements of the 50 million women across the nation
        whose lives have been influenced by Girl Scouting in the organization's first one
        hundred years.

2012   March 12: The one hundredth anniversary of GSUSA is celebrated.

SOURCE NOTES

Complete information for these source notes can be found in the bibliography. I've used some common abbreviations:

Choate: Anne Hyde Choate and Helen Ferris, *Juliette Low and the Girl Scouts: The Story of an American Woman, 1860–1927*

FHQ: Girl Scouts of Historic Georgia, First Headquarters, in Savannah, GA

GHS: Georgia Historical Society, in Savannah, GA

GGUK: Girlguiding UK

JGLB: Girl Scouts of the USA, Juliette Gordon Low Birthplace, in Savannah, GA

NHPC: Girl Scouts of the USA, National Historic Preservation Center, in New York City

Shultz: Gladys Denny Shultz and Daisy Gordon Lawrence, *Lady from Savannah: The Life of Juliette Low*

Schriner: Gertrude Schriner and Margaret Rogers, *Daisy's Chicago Heritage*

UNC: University of North Carolina, Gordon Family Papers

INTRODUCTION

PAGE

xi   *Loving one another . . .*: This is not a direct quote, but a summary of phrases, or
              paraphrases, based on Daisy's correspondence and speeches over the years.

CHAPTER ONE – LOVE AND WAR CLOUDS

2   "looked just like . . .": Shultz, p. 53.

3   "steal the show": Shultz, p. 11.

4   "I found that I really care . . .": Shultz, p. 54.

6   "never were the same in Savannah . . .": Shultz, p. 19.

6   "charming mischief-maker": Schriner, p. 24.

7   "I bet she's going to be a 'Daisy'": Shultz, p. 67.

CHAPTER TWO — THE CIVIL WAR

13   "I can even now feel the thrill . . .": Choate ("When I Was a Girl" by Juliette Low), p. 3.

15   "I suppose my father did it . . .": Letter from Nellie Gordon to *Ladies Home Journal*, November 25, 1914 (GHS).

15   "They came to my house frequently . . .": Shultz, p. 87.

16   "I've got a papa . . .": Shultz, p. 90.

CHAPTER THREE — CHICAGO AND RECONSTRUCTION

17   "that nice little beefsteak . . .": Schriner, p. 35.

17   "sweet and lovely [girl]": Shultz, p. 68.

18   "took up our stand . . .": Shultz, p. 90.

18   "For a long time after . . .": Shultz, p. 90.

18   "The war is over! . . .": Shultz, p. 99.

18   "We've won . . .": Shultz, p. 99.

19   "Where did it go?": Shultz, p. 91.

20   "This army has surrendered . . .": Shultz, p. 93.

20   "You'd best stay on in Chicago . . .": Shultz, p. 93.

25   According to one source . . .: Shultz, pp. 102–3.

CHAPTER FOUR — SUMMERS AND SCHOOLS

27   "There's just no use in me . . .": Shultz, p. 46.

27   "Well, it's not my fault . . .": Shultz, p. 119.

27   "It is hard to pay attention . . .": Shultz, p. 124.

27   "spittosporum": Shultz, p. 107.

28   "This very day . . .": Shultz, p. 107.

31   "My dear little Daisy": Shultz, p. 108.

36   "Please, don't try to manage *everything* . . .": Shultz, p. 160.

36   "I wore my white French muslin overskirt . . .": Shultz, p. 145.

CHAPTER FIVE – AT THE CLIFFS

37   "up-the-country": "Juliette Low: Juliette Low's School Days" by Daisy Gordon Lawrence, *The American Girl,* November 1938, p. 10.

38   "only the tip of her sharp little nose . . .": Choate ("Twenty Cousins in the Summer-Time" by Caroline Stiles Lovell), p. 20.

39   "circus trunk . . . filled with . . .": Shultz, p. 23.

39   "I was passing by a pig-sty . . .": Choate ("Twenty Cousins in the Summer-Time" by Caroline Stiles Lovell), p. 24.

39   "Dear [Mamma], we have such a nice time . . .": Letter from JGL to her mother in 1873, not dated (NHPC).

41   "had ledges at various heights . . .": Choate ("Twenty Cousins in the Summer-Time" by Caroline Stiles Lovell), p. 23.

41   "adored acting . . .": Choate ("Twenty Cousins in the Summer-Time" by Caroline Stiles Lovell), p. 21.

43   "Sister, you looked . . .": Choate ("When I Was a Girl" by Juliette Low), p. 7.

43   "its object was to help others": Choate ("When I Was a Girl" by Juliette Low), p. 6.

43   "did not know how to sew herself!": Choate ("Twenty Cousins in the Summer-Time" by Caroline Stiles Lovell), p. 15.

43   "Our first job was . . .": Juliette Low's annual birthday message, *The American Girl,*
      October 1926, p. 10.

44   "had great fun in [their] club . . .": Choate ("When I Was a Girl" by Juliette Low), pp. 6–7.

CHAPTER SIX – FINISHING SCHOOL

48   "You don't know how I love you . . .": Shultz, p. 145.

48   "There were no games . . .": Choate ("Daisy Goes to Boarding School" by Abby Lippitt Hunter), p. 30.

50   "Boys were equally unwelcome . . .": Choate ("Daisy Goes to Boarding School" by Abby Lippitt
      Hunter), p. 30.

51   "Can you realize . . ." "just precisely . . .": Shultz, p. 145.

53   "was not only very entertaining . . .": Choate ("As Her Family Knew Her" by G. Arthur Gordon), p. 42.

53   "How can you so desecrate the dead!": Shultz, p. 151.

CHAPTER SEVEN – LOVE AND MARRIAGE

56   "You probably have not thought my grief . . .": Shultz, p. 156.

57   "I am so glad you and Papa . . .": Shultz, p. 158.

58   "He is a dear little dog . . .": Shultz, p. 159.

58   "The waters do her good . . .": Shultz, p. 159.

59   "[Willy] does not even know . . .": Shultz, p. 163.

59   "I don't feel in the least afraid . . .": Shultz, p. 161.

60   "And now you will probably keep me . . .": Shultz, p. 167.

60   "I had [had] a series of ear infections . . .": www.scoutingweb.com.

61   "so nervous to being distracted": Shultz, p. 169.

62   "My dear Capt. Gordon . . .": Shultz, p. 172.

62   "I am to live in Savannah . . .": Shultz, p. 173.

62   "as good as engaged": Shultz, p. 163.

64   "I am glad Willy was ashamed . . .": Letter to Daisy from her father, September 3, 1886 (JGLB).

65   "sash . . . looped with an elegant . . .": *Savannah Morning News*, December 22, 1886.

CHAPTER EIGHT — EUROPE

68   "it was simpler . . .": Shultz, p. 198.

72   "I let him fly about the drawing room . . .": Letter from Daisy in 1890 (JGLB).

73   "I wore all my diamonds . . .": Letter from Daisy in May 1889 (JGLB).

73   "It took us until six to walk . . .": Letter from Daisy in May 1889 (JGLB).

74   "'look out for number one,'": Shultz, p. 187.

74   "I felt exactly as if I were bowing . . .": Letter from Daisy in May 1889 (JGLB).

77   "cut from sheets of the copper . . .": "1942 recollections" by Eleanor Wayne McPherson (NHPC).

77   "I developed the muscles of my right arm . . .": "More About Juliette Gordon Low" by Alix Liddell, *The Guide*, April 22, 1949.

77   "One thing I want very much . . .": Shultz, p. 192.

77   "I keep thinking all day and dreaming all night . . .": Shultz, p. 193.

79   "like Scotch weather . . .": Shultz, pp. 232–33.

CHAPTER NINE — WARS

80   "I think it is all *wrong*. . . .": Shultz, p. 214.

83   "positive disgrace": Shultz, p. 218.

84   "to her very finger tips": Choate ("As Her Family Knew Her" by G. Arthur Gordon), pp. 41–42.

84   "Daisy is working like a brick": Shultz, p. 220.

86   "annoyed at something . . .": Shultz, p. 232.

86   "managed" Papa: Schulz, p. 233.

86   "I see so little of Billow . . .": Shultz, p. 233.

87   "our Daisy" or "our little Daisy": Shultz, p. 233.

87   "Happiness is not the sum total . . .": Shultz, p. 234.

88   "How could anyone possibly blame . . .": Shultz, p. 239.

88   "neither maid, wife, or widow": Shultz, p. 243.

88   "Divorce [is] wrong . . .": Shultz, pp. 242–43.

89   "for the sake of those years . . .": Shultz, p. 251.

89   "All my money bothers are now . . .": Shultz, p. 259.

89   "held out kind hands . . .": Shultz, p. 259.

89   "Hello Peggy, I have just arrived back . . .": "In Proud Memory of My Aunt Juliette Gordon Low" by Peggy Graves, not dated, p. 1 (NHPC).

91   "brooded over the fact . . .": Choate ("As Her Family Knew Her" by G. Arthur Gordon), pp. 59–60.

CHAPTER TEN — A LIFE-CHANGING LUNCHEON

93   "My own father and brothers . . .": Shultz, p. 264.

93   "This Year" . . . "Never": Choate ("Our Delightful Companion" by Rowland Leigh), p. 149.

93   "Wait to get your income . . .": Shultz, p. 271.

93   "You are not only making . . ." "I do hope . . .": Shultz, p. 269.

93   "It comes and goes like the fog.": Interview with Katherine Keena (JGLB).

94   "It was a tricky device . . .": "My Aunt Daisy Was the First Girl Scout" by Arthur Gordon, *Woman's Day*, March 1956, p. 111.

94   "warm brown eyes . . .": "My Aunt Daisy Was the First Girl Scout" by Arthur Gordon,
        Woman's Day, March 1956, p. 33.

95   "With delightful recollections . . .": Gordon House Guest Book (JGLB).

97   "while brushing her teeth . . .": Shultz, pp. 87–88.

97   "I find friends everywhere.": Shultz, p. 290.

97   "I am just an idle woman . . .": Shultz, p. 260.

97   "The road which led from you to me": Choate ("As Her Family Knew Her" by G. Arthur
        Gordon), p. 58.

97   "modeling": Shultz, p. 288.

98   "Much of her work reveals real power . . .": Choate ("As Her Family Knew Her" by
        G. Arthur Gordon), pp. 57–58.

100   "The impression he makes on one . . .": Juliette Gordon Low journal, May 30, 1911 (JGLB).

100   "A sort of intuition comes over me . . .": Juliette Gordon Low journal, June 1, 1911 (JGLB).

102   "No doubt about his magnetism. . . .": Juliette Gordon Low journal, June 17, 1911 (JGLB).

CHAPTER ELEVEN – AN IDEA FOR ALL OF AMERICA

104   "The Girl Guides is a sort of outcome . . .": Shultz, p. 299.

105   "Girls must be partners and comrades . . .": Girl Guides of Canada, Fact Sheet, "The Three
        Baden-Powells: Robert, Agnes and Olave," p. 4.

105   "I am getting up a corp[s] of Girl Guides here . . .": Shultz, p. 300.

108   "'Then that is settled' . . .": Choate ("Juliette Low Meets Sir Robert Baden-Powell and
        the Girl Guides" by Rose Kerr), p. 69.

108   "And I should like you to give them . . .": Choate ("Juliette Low Meets Sir Robert
        Baden-Powell and the Girl Guides" by Rose Kerr), p. 70.

109   "genius for not hearing any excuses . . .": Choate ("Juliette Low Meets Sir Robert
       Baden-Powell and the Girl Guides" by Rose Kerr), p. 71.

109   "the seeds of the Girl Guide movement . . .": Choate ("Daisy Low as I Remember Her"
       by Olave Baden-Powell), p. 195.

110   "There was something magnetic about her . . .": Transcript of Olave Baden-Powell
       recording, 1968, p. 1 (GGUK).

110   "There we met on board ship . . .": Transcript of Olave Baden-Powell recording, 1968, p. 1 (GGUK).

111   "Imagine a woman, delicate . . .": Choate ("Juliette Low Meets Sir Robert Baden-Powell
       and the Girl Guides" by Rose Kerr), p. 70.

112   "a moth-eaten specimen . . .": "My Aunt Daisy Was the First Girl Scout" by Arthur Gordon,
       Woman's Day, March 1956, p. 110.

113   "Come right over . . .": Choate ("Juliette Low Brings Girl Scouting to the United States"
       by Edith D. Johnston), p. 82.

CHAPTER TWELVE — LAUNCHING A DREAM

116   "I may become . . .": Letter from Daisy to her mother, March 2, 1912 (JGLB).

116   "I am deep in Girl Guides . . .": Letter from Daisy to her sister Mabel, March 12, 1912 (UNC).

117   "Here are the girls. . . .": Choate ("Juliette Low Brings Girl Scouting to the United States"
       by Edith D. Johnston), pp. 82–83.

117   "'You've made me a what?' . . .": Shultz, p. 308.

118   "sitting perched on a high stool . . .": "Juliette Low: Juliette Low as I Knew Her" by Daisy
       Gordon Lawrence, *The American Girl,* October 1938, p. 5.

120   "We played games . . .": Choate ("Juliette Low Brings Girl Scouting to the United States"
       by Edith D. Johnston), p. 83.

121   "The rooms were packed with them . . .": Letter to Daisy from her father, May 14, 1912 (JGLB).

121   "filled with quaintly misspelled words": Choate ("Juliette Low Brings Girl Scouting to the
       United States" by Edith D. Johnston), p. 84.

CHAPTER THIRTEEN — THE DREAM BUILDS

123   "Her heart, kidneys, liver . . .": Shultz, p. 312.

124   "I don't think it helps to write . . ." "lost, in Papa . . ." : Shultz, p. 314.

126   "could tell ghost stories . . .": "Juliette Low: Juliette Low Grown Up" by Daisy Gordon Lawrence,
       The American Girl, December 1938, p. 19.

127   "Girls will do no good by trying to imitate boys. . . .": *How Girls Can Help Their Country:
       Handbook for Girl Scouts*, p. 12.

127   "welcome all obstacles . . .": "Juliette: In Her Own Words," *Leader*, Spring 2006, p. 27.

127   "I selected the name 'Scouts' because . . .": *Savannah Morning News*, not dated but probably
       February 1913 (JGLB).

128   The Girl Scout Promise and The Girl Scout Laws: *How Girls Can Help Their Country:
       Handbook for Girl Scouts*, pp. 3–6.

129   "I could not refuse her . . .": Choate ("Juliette Low Brings Girl Scouting to the United States"
       by Edith D. Johnston), pp. 86–87.

130   "give a [damn] . . .": Shultz, p. 322.

131   "a little old lady with snapping black eyes . . .": Shultz, p. 344.

131   "Everything is done up new . . .": Shultz, p. 331.

131   "Mam[m]a says she *likes* my . . .": Shultz, p. 331.

132   "I must save every penny . . .": Shultz, p. 342.

CHAPTER FOURTEEN — THE ORGANIZATION GROWS

135   "rushing through factories . . .": *Savannah Morning News,* May 7, 1916.

136   "Daisy's Scouts are booming! . . .": Shultz, p. 337.

136   "I do not know how she lives . . .": Shultz, p. 341.

136   "I never use the word . . .": Letter from Daisy to her mother, June 4, 1914 (JGLB).

136   "I want to arrive by the eighteenth . . .": Shultz, p. 341.

137   "motor": Shultz, p. 265.

137   "didn't think it would be polite . . .": Shultz, p. 266.

138   "She had ways of her own in driving . . .": Letter from Rudyard Kipling to Arthur Gordon, October 14, 1928 (FHQ).

139   "just pin on badges . . .": Choate ("Girl Scouting Gets Under Way" by Anne Hyde Choate), p. 96.

139   "Well, you [had] . . . better accept the position . . .": Choate ("Girl Scouting Gets Under Way" by Anne Hyde Choate), p. 98.

140   "The girls must always come first": Shultz, p. 357.

140   "Oh, is my trimming sad? . . .": Shultz, p. 342.

141   "I have seen her come into a room . . .": Choate ("Adventuring in Egypt with Daisy" by Eleanor Nash McWilliams), pp. 153–54.

141   "I'm not dead yet!": Shultz, p. 346.

141   "I didn't walk down the stairs . . .": Shultz, p. 347.

144   "quicksilver and pepper . . .": "Getting to Know Juliette Gordon Low" by Ed Levy, *Leader,* Fall/Winter, 2009.

145   "I can see from my front windows . . .": Shultz, p. 352.

CHAPTER FIFTEEN — BUSY ON BEHALF OF GIRL SCOUTS

147   "Everyone [in England] dances . . .": Shultz, p. 353.

147   "the greatest surprise of my life. . . .": Message from Daisy to Girl Scouts (GHS).

148   "*loved* her whole uniform": Shultz, p. 351.

148   "the Girl Scout literature . . .": Choate ("Girl Scouting Gets Under Way" by Anne Hyde Choate), p. 103.

148   "hard to straighten her out" "rarest of human beings . . .": Shultz, p. 356.

148   "I realize that each year it has changed . . .": Daisy's annual birthday message, *The American Girl*, October 1925, p. 11.

149   "Girl Scouting, to Daisy . . .": "My Aunt Daisy Was the First Girl Scout" by Arthur Gordon, *Woman's Day*, March 1956, p. 111.

151   "so that mothers . . .": "An Anniversary to Remember" by Susan Einarson, *Girl Scout Leader*, Summer 1995, p. 28.

151   "going with us on our hikes . . .": Choate ("Juliette Low Goes Camping" by Dorris Hough), pp. 111–12.

151   "she read the palm of every person . . .": Choate ("Juliette Low Goes Camping" by Dorris Hough), p. 112.

152   "dashed out . . .": *Savannah Morning News*, April 13, 1922.

152   "I did not realize when the first patrol . . .": Daisy's speech notes, May 1922 (GHS).

152   "A few years ago in my ignorance . . .": Daisy's speech notes, May 1922 (GHS).

153   "My Dear Girl Scouts, Little did I dream . . .": Daisy's annual birthday message, *The American Girl*, October 1923, p. 13.

153   "To put yourself in another's place . . .": Daisy's annual birthday message, *The American Girl*, October 1923, p. 13.

154 "I look forward to seeing the parents . . .": Shultz, p. 362.

154 "mean nothing in themselves . . ." "Scouting is the cradle . . .": *Leader,* Spring 2006, p. 27.

155 "Aunt Daisy confided to me . . .": "In Proud Memory of My Aunt Juliette Gordon Low" by Peggy Graves, not dated, p. 9 (NHPC).

156 "Darling Peggie, Don't imagine . . .": "In Proud Memory of My Aunt Juliette Gordon Low" by Peggy Graves, not dated, p. 8 (NHPC).

CHAPTER SIXTEEN — CAMP MACY

157 "Hullo Peggy, I'm home . . .": "In Proud Memory of My Aunt Juliette Gordon Low" by Peggy Graves, not dated, p. 9 (NHPC).

157 "Champagne is for parties . . .": "In Proud Memory of My Aunt Juliette Gordon Low" by Peggy Graves, not dated, p. 10 (NHPC).

158 "spent each day with her . . .": "In Proud Memory of My Aunt Juliette Gordon Low" by Peggy Graves, not dated, p. 12 (NHPC).

158 "Every place I visit . . .": Shultz, p. 365.

158 "enrolled Mrs. Coolidge as a Girl Scout! . . .": Shultz, p. 365.

159 "Why, so I am! . . .": Shultz, p. 265.

159 "I have a wonderful new plan! . . .": Shultz, pp. 365–67.

160 "without stopping once, the traffic . . .": Choate ("The World Camp" by Mary Lagercrantz), p. 184.

162 "strolled along the sandy lane . . .": Choate ("Daisy Low as I Remember Her" by Olave Baden-Powell), p. 195.

162 "We bowed the plasterers out . . .": Choate ("Her Dream Comes True" by Jane Deeter Rippin), p. 169.

164 "Let her alone. If she wanted . . .": Transcript of speech by Arthur Gordon at the Juliette Low Dinner, Conference of Girl Scouts of Region Three, April 30, 1935, p. 8 (NHPC).

164 "We mustn't lose sight of the girls.": Shultz, p. 357.

164 "I have a wonderful plan . . .": Shultz, p. 377.

165 "Daisy has only six weeks to live.": Shultz, p. 377.

165 "There won't be any left for the funeral . . .": Shultz, p. 378.

165 "[Aunt Daisy] was always . . .": "My Aunt Daisy Was the First Girl Scout" by Arthur Gordon, *Woman's Day,* March 1956, p. 33.

165 "I trust I have left no enmities . . .": Shultz, p. 379.

165 "How nice it is to believe . . .": Letter from Daisy to Mary Gale Carter, January 16, 1927 (JGLB).

166 "stood at attention and saluted . . .": "In Proud Memory of My Aunt Juliette Gordon Low" by Peggy Graves, not dated, p. 15 (NHPC).

167 "You are not only the first Girl Scout . . .": Shultz, p. 378.

CHAPTER SEVENTEEN - A BIG LITTLE WOMAN'S LEGACY

171 The Girl Scout Promise and The Girl Scout Law: Copyright GSUSA.

172 "Girl Scouting builds girls of courage . . .": Copyright GSUSA.

177 "a big little woman": Choate ("Here and There with Juliette Low in Girl Scouting" by Josephine Daskam Bacon), p. 138.

177 "dauntless little Joan of Arc . . .": Choate ("Here and There with Juliette Low in Girl Scouting" by Josephine Daskam Bacon), p. 138.

BIBLIOGRAPHY

BOOKS:

FOR ADULTS

Biegert, Melissa Ann Langley. "*Woman Scout: The Empowerment of Juliette Gordon Low.*" PhD dissertation, University of Texas at Austin, 1998.

Choate, Anne Hyde, and Helen Ferris, eds. *Juliette Low and the Girl Scouts: The Story of An American Woman, 1860–1927.* New York: Girl Scouts National Organization, first published in 1928. A collection of stories, poems, letters, and recollections written by Juliette Low or about her by her family, friends, or Girl Scouts.

Cordery, Stacy A. *Juliette Gordon Low: The Remarkable Founder of the Girl Scouts.* New York: Viking, 2012.

Degenhardt, Mary, and Judith Kirsch. *Girl Scout Collector's Guide: A History of Uniforms, Insignia, Publications, and Memorabilia.* Lubbock: Texas Tech University Press, 2005.

Hoxie, W. J. *How Girls Can Help Their Country: Handbook for Girl Scouts.* Bedford, Mass.: Applewood Books, not dated. Originally written and published in 1913 by Juliette Low.

Kinzie, Mrs. J. H. *Wau-Bun: The "Early-Day" in the North-West.* New York: National Society of Colonial Dames in Wisconsin, 1975. Originally published in 1856.

Schriner, Gertrude, and Margaret Rogers. *Daisy's Chicago Heritage.* Vernon Hills, Ill.: Girl Scouts-Illinois Crossroads Council, 1976.

Shultz, Gladys Denny, and Daisy Gordon Lawrence. *Lady from Savannah: The Life of Juliette Low.* New York: Girl Scouts of the USA, first published in 1958. Daisy Gordon Lawrence was a niece of Juliette Gordon Low's.

Bibliography

FOR YOUNG READERS

Aller, Susan Bivin. *Juliette Low*. Minneapolis: Lerner Publications, 2007.

Brown, Fern. *Daisy and the Girl Scouts*. Morton Grove, Ill.: Albert Whitman, 1996.

Fradin, Judith Bloom, and Dennis Brindell Fradin. *Jane Addams: Champion of Democracy*. New York: Clarion, 2006.

Freedman, Russell. *Lincoln: A Photobiography*. New York: Clarion, 1987.

———. *The War to End All Wars: World War I*. New York: Clarion, 2010.

Kudlinski, Kathleen V. *Juliette Gordon Low: America's First Girl Scout*. (Women of Our Time). New York: Viking Press, 1988.

Pace, Mildred Mastin. *Juliette Low*. New York: Charles Scribner's Sons, 1947. This out-of-print biography was written in gratitude to Mrs. Samuel C. Lawrence, Juliette Gordon Low's niece and namesake.

Peavy, Linda, and Ursula Smith. *Dreams into Deeds: Nine Women Who Dared*. New York: Charles Scribner's Sons, 1985.

MAGAZINES, NEWSPAPERS, GIRL SCOUT HANDOUTS, AND MISCELLANEOUS

Bagnall, Ralph. "Girl Scouts Founder Was Also a Woodworker." *Woodworker's Journal*, June 2007.

Clancy, Jacqueline E. "Hell's Angel: Eleanor Kinzie Gordon's Wartime Summer of 1898." *Tequesta* 63, 2003.

Edmondson, Jolee. "Scout's Honor: Juliette Gordon Low and the Founding of the Girl Scouts." *Delta Sky*, February 2003, pp. 68, 70–71.

Einarson, Susan. "An Anniversary to Remember." *Girl Scout Leader*, Summer 1995, p. 28.

Gordon, Arthur. "My Aunt Daisy Was the First Girl Scout." *Woman's Day*, March 1956, pp. 33, 109–14.

Bibliography

Graves, Peggy. "In Proud Memory of My Aunt Juliette Gordon Low." Girl Scouts of the USA, National Historic Preservation Center, New York, N.Y., not dated.

LaPorte, Léo F. "Lou Henry Hoover: A Woman of Independent Thinking." University of California, Santa Cruz, CA, not dated. Girl Scouts of the USA, National Historic Preservation Center, New York, N.Y.

Lawrence, Daisy Gordon. "Juliette Low." *The American Girl,* serialized in October, November, and December 1938.

Levy, Ed. "Getting to Know Juliette Gordon Low." *Leader,* Fall/Winter, 2009.

Liddell, Alix. "More About Juliette Gordon Low." *The Guide,* April 22, 1949.

Low, Juliette Gordon. Birthday Message, *The American Girl,* October 1923, p. 13.

———. Birthday Message. *The American Girl,* October 1924, p. 11.

———. Birthday Message. *The American Girl,* October 1925, p. 11.

———. Birthday Message. *The American Girl,* October 1926, p. 10.

Lyon, Nancy. "Juliette Low: The Eccentric Who Founded the Girl Scouts." *Ms. Magazine,* November 1981.

McPherson, Eleanor Wayne. "1942 recollections." Girl Scouts of the USA, National Historic Preservation Center, New York, N.Y.

Savannah Morning News. Various dates.

Saxton, Martha. "The Best Girl Scout of Them All." *American Heritage,* June/July 1982, pp. 38–46.

Staff editors. "Juliette: In Her Own Words." *Leader,* Spring 2006.

WEBSITES

Andrew Low House: www.andrewlowhouse.com

Girl Guides of Canada: www.girlguides.ca

Bibliography

Girlguiding UK: www.girlguiding.org.uk

Girl Scouts of Historic Georgia: www.gshg.org

Girl Scouts of the USA: www.girlscouts.org

Juliette Gordon Low Birthplace: www.juliettegordonlowbirthplace.org

World Association of Girl Guides and Girl Scouts: www.wagggsworld.org

OTHER SOURCES

Baden-Powell, Olave. Transcript of recording. 1968. Courtesy of the Girl Guides,
    United Kingdom.

Gordon, George Arthur. Transcript of speech given at the Juliette Low Dinner of the Conference
    of Girl Scouts of Region Three. Richmond, Va., April 30, 1935.

Lawrence, Daisy Gordon, and Ethel Rusk Dermady. Transcript of conversation. Savannah, Ga.,
    December 1965. Girl Scouts of the USA, National Historic Preservation Center, New York, N.Y.

PLACES TO VISIT IN THE UNITED STATES

Andrew Low House, Savannah, Ga.

Georgia Historical Society, Savannah, Ga.

Girl Scouts of Historic Georgia, First Headquarters, Savannah, Ga.

Girl Scouts of the USA, National Historic Preservation Center, New York N.Y.

Juliette Gordon Low Birthplace, Savannah, Ga.

University of North Carolina at Chapel Hill, archive of the Gordon Family Papers, 1810–1968.

INDEX

Page numbers in **boldface** indicate illustrations.